Bilingual
VISUAL
dictionary

Bilingual

VISUAL

dictionary

Senior Editor Angeles Gavira
Senior Art Editor Ina Stradins
DTP Designers Sunil Sharma, Balwant Singh,
Harish Aggarwal, John Goldsmid, Ashwani Tyagi
DTP Coordinator Pankaj Sharma
Production Controller Liz Cherry
Picture Researcher Anna Grapes
Managing Editor Liz Wheeler
Managing Art Editor Phil Ormerod
Category Publisher Jonathan Metcalf

Designed for Dorling Kindersley by WaltonCreative.com
Art Editor Colin Walton, assisted by Tracy Musson
Designers Peter Radcliffe, Earl Neish, Ann Cannings
Picture Research Marissa Keating

Language content for Dorling Kindersley by
g-and-w PUBLISHING
Managed by Jane Wightwick, assisted by Ana Bremón
Translation and editing by Christine Arthur
Additional input by Dr. Arturo Pretel, Martin Prill,
Frédéric Monteil, Meinrad Prill, Mari Bremón,
Oscar Bremón, Anunchi Bremón, Leila Gaafar

First published in Great Britain in 2005
This revised edition published in 2015 by
Dorling Kindersley Limited,
80 Strand, London WC2R 0RL

A Penguin Random House Company

Content first published as
5 Language Visual Dictionary in 2003

2 4 6 8 10 9 7 5 3
003 – BD219 – June/15

A CIP catalogue record for this
book is available from the British Library.
ISBN: 978-0-2411-9920-6

Printed in China

A WORLD OF IDEAS:
SEE ALL THERE IS TO KNOW

www.dk.com

contenido
contents

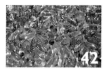

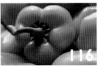

CONTENIDO • CONTENTS

comer fuera •
eating out

el estudio • study

el trabajo • work

el transporte •
transport

los deportes • sport

el ocio • leisure

el medio ambiente
• environment

los datos • reference

sobre el diccionario

Está comprobado que el empleo de fotografías ayuda a la comprensión y a la retención de información. Basados en este principio, este diccionario bilingüe y altamente ilustrado exhibe un amplio registro de vocabulario útil y actual en dos idiomas europeos.

El diccionario aparece dividido según su temática y abarca la mayoría de los aspectos del mundo cotidiano con detalle, desde el restaurante al gimnasio, la casa al lugar de trabajo, el espacio al reino animal. Encontrará también palabras y frases adicionales para su uso en conversación y para ampliar su vocabulario.

Este diccionario es un instrumento de referencia esencial para todo aquél que esté interesado en los idiomas; es práctico, estimulante y fácil de usar.

Algunos puntos a observar

Los dos idiomas se presentan siempre en el mismo orden: español e inglés.

En español, los sustantivos se muestran con sus artículos definidos reflejando el género (masculino o femenino) y el número (singular/plural):

la semilla   **las almendras**
seed   almonds

Los verbos se indican con una (v) después del inglés:

recolectar • harvest (v)

Cada idioma tiene su propio índice. Aquí podrá mirar una palabra en cualquiera de los dos idiomas y se le indicará el número de la página donde aparece. El género se indica utilizando las siguientes abreviaturas:

m = masculino
f = femenino

about the dictionary

The use of pictures is proven to aid understanding and the retention of information. Working on this principle, this highly-illustrated bilingual dictionary presents a large range of useful current vocabulary in two European languages.

The dictionary is divided thematically and covers most aspects of the everyday world in detail, from the restaurant to the gym, the home to the workplace, outer space to the animal kingdom. You will also find additional words and phrases for conversational use and for extending your vocabulary.

This is an essential reference tool for anyone interested in languages – practical, stimulating, and easy-to-use.

A few things to note

The two languages are always presented in the same order – Spanish and English.

In Spanish, nouns are given with their definite articles reflecting the gender (masculine or feminine) and number (singular or plural), for example:

la semilla   **las almendras**
seed   almonds

Verbs are indicated by a (v) after the English, for example:

recolectar • harvest (v)

Each language also has its own index at the back of the book. Here you can look up a word in either of the two languages and be referred to the page number(s) where it appears. The gender is shown using the following abbreviations:

m = masculine
f = feminine

cómo utilizar este libro

how to use this book

Ya se encuentre aprendiendo un idioma nuevo por motivos de trabajo, placer, o para preparar sus vacaciones al extranjero, o ya quiera ampliar su vocabulario en un idioma que ya conoce, este diccionario es un instrumento muy valioso que podrá utilizar de distintas maneras.

Cuando esté aprendiendo un idioma nuevo, busque palabras similares en distintos idiomas y palabras que parecen similares pero que poseen significados totalmente distintos. También podrá observar cómo los idiomas se influyen unos a otros. Por ejemplo, la lengua inglesa ha importado muchos términos de comida de otras lenguas pero, a cambio, ha exportado términos empleados en tecnología y cultura popular.

Whether you are learning a new language for business, pleasure, or in preparation for a holiday abroad, or are hoping to extend your vocabulary in an already familiar language, this dictionary is a valuable learning tool which you can use in a number of different ways.

When learning a new language, look out for cognates (words that are alike in different languages) and false friends (words that look alike but carry significantly different meanings). You can also see where the languages have influenced each other. For example, English has imported many terms for food from other European languages but, in turn, exported terms used in technology and popular culture.

Actividades prácticas de aprendizaje

• Mientras se desplaza por su casa, lugar de trabajo o colegio, intente mirar las páginas que se refieren a ese lugar. Podrá entonces cerrar el libro, mirar a su alrededor y ver cuántos objetos o características puede nombrar.

• Desafíese a usted mismo a escribir una historia, carta o diálogo empleando tantos términos de una página concreta como le sea posible. Esto le ayudará a retener vocabulario y recordar la ortografía. Si quiere ir progresando para poder escribir un texto más largo, comience con frases que incorporen 2 ó 3 palabras.

• Si tiene buena memoria visual, intente dibujar o calcar objetos del libro; luego cierre el libro y escriba las palabras correspondientes debajo del dibujo.

• Cuando se sienta más seguro, escoja palabras del índice de uno de los idiomas y vea si sabe lo que significan antes de consultar la página correspondiente para comprobarlo.

Practical learning activities

• As you move about your home, workplace, or college, try looking at the pages which cover that setting. You could then close the book, look around you and see how many of the objects and features you can name.

• Challenge yourself to write a story, letter, or dialogue using as many of the terms on a particular page as possible. This will help you retain the vocabulary and remember the spelling. If you want to build up to writing a longer text, start with sentences incorporating 2–3 words.

• If you have a very visual memory, try drawing or tracing items from the book onto a piece of paper, then close the book and fill in the words below the picture.

• Once you are more confident, pick out words in a foreign-language index and see if you know what they mean before turning to the relevant page to check if you were right.

la gente
people

el cuerpo • body

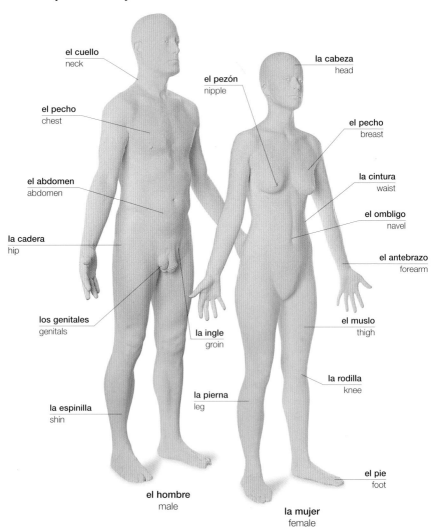

el cuello
neck

el pezón
nipple

la cabeza
head

el pecho
chest

el pecho
breast

la cintura
waist

el abdomen
abdomen

el ombligo
navel

la cadera
hip

el antebrazo
forearm

los genitales
genitals

la ingle
groin

el muslo
thigh

la rodilla
knee

la pierna
leg

la espinilla
shin

el pie
foot

el hombre
male

la mujer
female

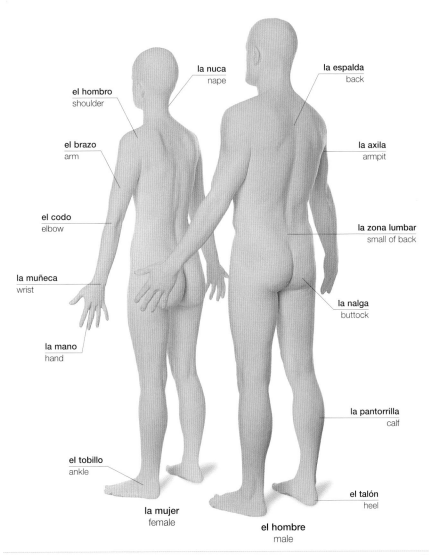

la nuca
nape

la espalda
back

el hombro
shoulder

el brazo
arm

la axila
armpit

el codo
elbow

la zona lumbar
small of back

la muñeca
wrist

la nalga
buttock

la mano
hand

la pantorrilla
calf

el tobillo
ankle

el talón
heel

la mujer
female

el hombre
male

la cara • face

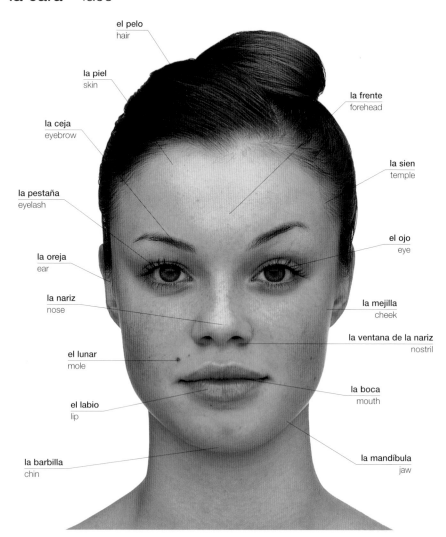

el pelo
hair

la piel
skin

la frente
forehead

la ceja
eyebrow

la sien
temple

la pestaña
eyelash

el ojo
eye

la oreja
ear

la mejilla
cheek

la nariz
nose

la ventana de la nariz
nostril

el lunar
mole

la boca
mouth

el labio
lip

la barbilla
chin

la mandíbula
jaw

la arruga
wrinkle

la peca
freckle

el poro
pore

el hoyuelo
dimple

la mano • hand

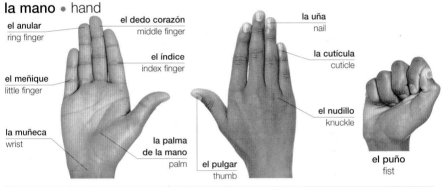

el anular
ring finger

el dedo corazón
middle finger

el índice
index finger

el meñique
little finger

la muñeca
wrist

la palma de la mano
palm

la uña
nail

la cutícula
cuticle

el nudillo
knuckle

el pulgar
thumb

el puño
fist

el pie • foot

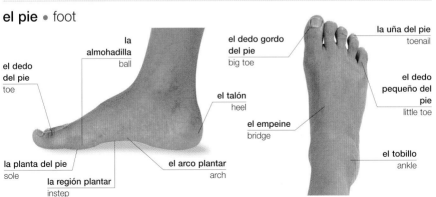

la almohadilla
ball

el dedo del pie
toe

el talón
heel

la planta del pie
sole

la región plantar
instep

el arco plantar
arch

el dedo gordo del pie
big toe

el empeine
bridge

la uña del pie
toenail

el dedo pequeño del pie
little toe

el tobillo
ankle

los músculos • muscles

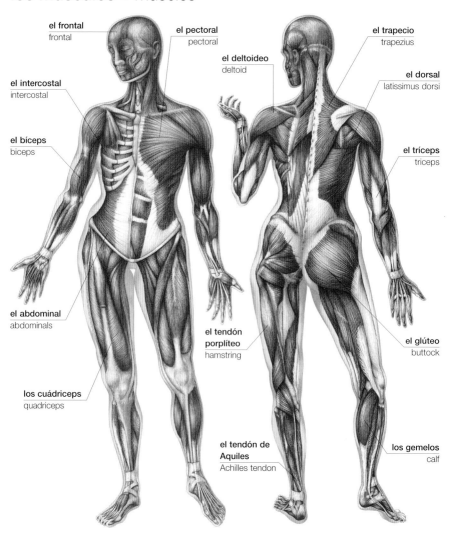

el frontal
frontal

el pectoral
pectoral

el trapecio
trapezius

el deltoideo
deltoid

el dorsal
latissimus dorsi

el intercostal
intercostal

el bíceps
biceps

el tríceps
triceps

el abdominal
abdominals

el tendón
porplíteo
hamstring

el glúteo
buttock

los cuádriceps
quadriceps

el tendón de
Aquiles
Achilles tendon

los gemelos
calf

el esqueleto • skeleton

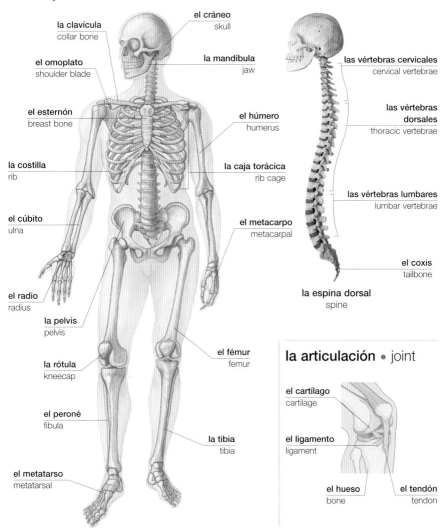

la clavícula
collar bone

el cráneo
skull

la mandíbula
jaw

el omoplato
shoulder blade

el esternón
breast bone

el húmero
humerus

la costilla
rib

la caja torácica
rib cage

el cúbito
ulna

el metacarpo
metacarpal

el radio
radius

la pelvis
pelvis

la rótula
kneecap

el fémur
femur

el peroné
fibula

la tibia
tibia

el metatarso
metatarsal

las vértebras cervicales
cervical vertebrae

las vértebras
dorsales
thoracic vertebrae

las vértebras lumbares
lumbar vertebrae

el coxis
tailbone

la espina dorsal
spine

la articulación • joint

el cartílago
cartilage

el ligamento
ligament

el hueso
bone

el tendón
tendon

los órganos internos • internal organs

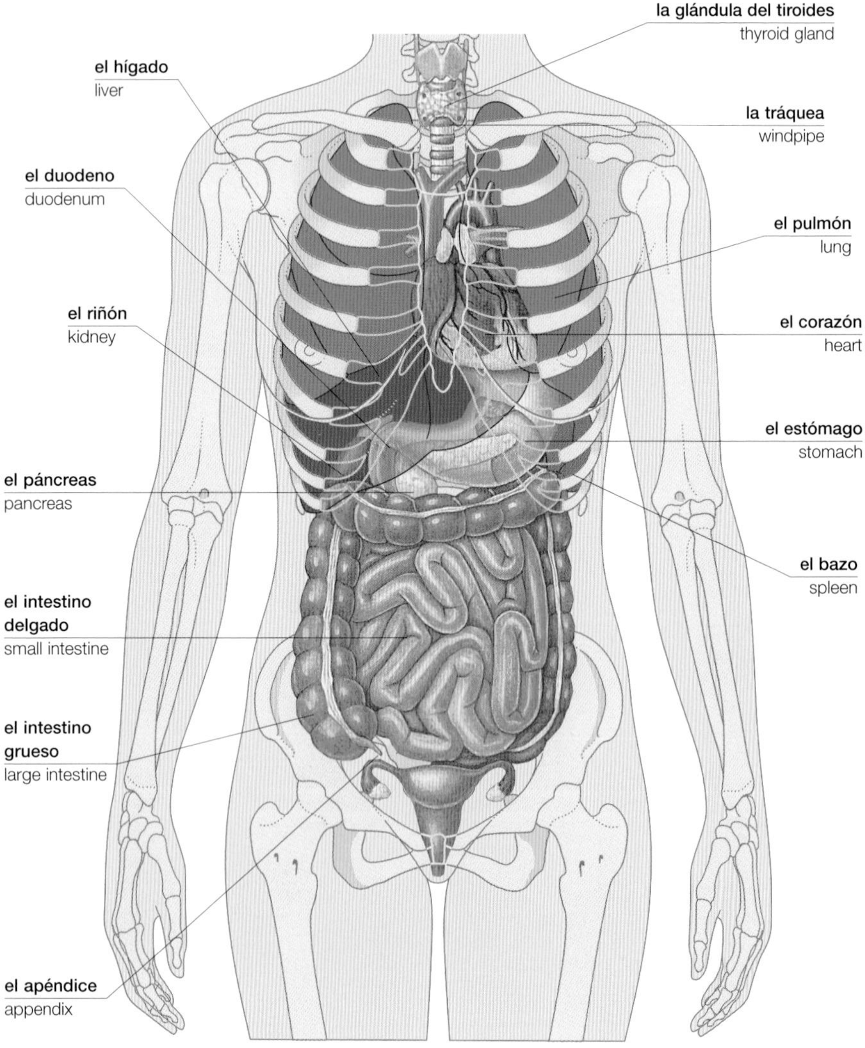

la glándula del tiroides
thyroid gland

el hígado
liver

la tráquea
windpipe

el duodeno
duodenum

el pulmón
lung

el riñón
kidney

el corazón
heart

el páncreas
pancreas

el estómago
stomach

el bazo
spleen

el intestino
delgado
small intestine

el intestino
grueso
large intestine

el apéndice
appendix

la cabeza • head

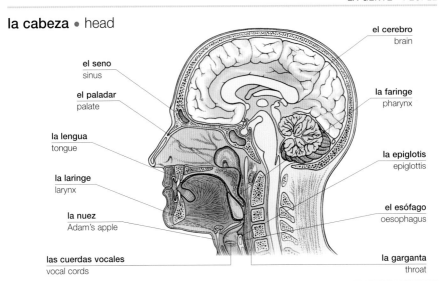

el cerebro
brain

el seno
sinus

el paladar
palate

la lengua
tongue

la laringe
larynx

la nuez
Adam's apple

las cuerdas vocales
vocal cords

la faringe
pharynx

la epiglotis
epiglottis

el esófago
oesophagus

la garganta
throat

los sistemas • body systems

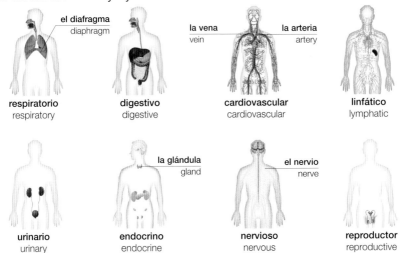

el diafragma
diaphragm

respiratorio
respiratory

digestivo
digestive

la vena
vein

la arteria
artery

cardiovascular
cardiovascular

linfático
lymphatic

urinario
urinary

la glándula
gland

endocrino
endocrine

el nervio
nerve

nervioso
nervous

reproductor
reproductive

los órganos reproductores • reproductive organs

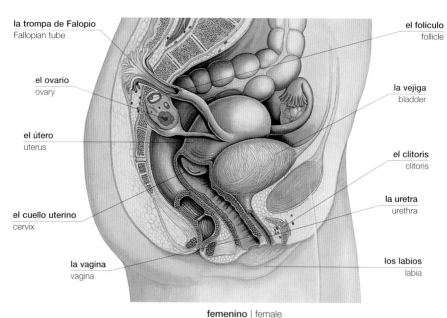

la trompa de Falopio
Fallopian tube

el ovario
ovary

el útero
uterus

el cuello uterino
cervix

la vagina
vagina

el folículo
follicle

la vejiga
bladder

el clítoris
clitoris

la uretra
urethra

los labios
labia

femenino | female

la reproducción • reproduction

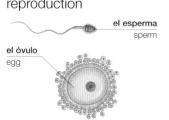

el esperma
sperm

el óvulo
egg

la fertilización | fertilization

vocabulario • vocabulary		
la hormona hormone	**impotente** impotent	**la menstruación** menstruation
la ovulación ovulation	**fértil** fertile	**el coito** intercourse
estéril infertile	**concebir** conceive	**la enfermedad de transmisión sexual** sexually transmitted disease

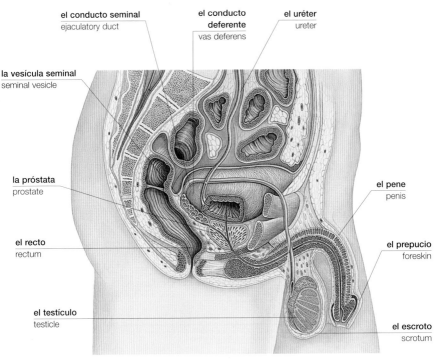

el conducto seminal
ejaculatory duct

el conducto deferente
vas deferens

el uréter
ureter

la vesícula seminal
seminal vesicle

la próstata
prostate

el pene
penis

el recto
rectum

el prepucio
foreskin

el testículo
testicle

el escroto
scrotum

masculino | male

la anticoncepción • contraception

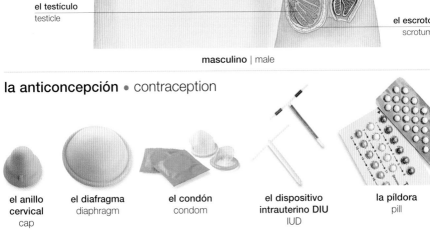

el anillo cervical
cap

el diafragma
diaphragm

el condón
condom

el dispositivo intrauterino DIU
IUD

la píldora
pill

la familia • family

la abuela
grandmother

el abuelo
grandfather

el tío
uncle

la tía
aunt

el padre
father

la madre
mother

el primo
cousin

el hermano
brother

la hermana
sister

la mujer
wife

la nuera
daughter-in-law

el hijo
son

la hija
daughter

el yerno
son-in-law

el nieto
grandson

la nieta
granddaughter

el marido
husband

vocabulario • vocabulary

los parientes	los padres	los nietos	la madrastra	el hijastro	la generación
relatives	parents	grandchildren	stepmother	stepson	generation

los abuelos	los niños	el padrastro	la hijastra	el/la compañero/-a	los gemelos
grandparents	children	stepfather	stepdaughter	partner	twins

la suegra
mother-in-law

el suegro
father-in-law

el cuñado
brother-in-law

la cuñada
sister-in-law

la sobrina
niece

el sobrino
nephew

Señorita
Miss

los tratamientos
• titles

Señora
Mrs

Señor
Mr

las etapas • stages

el bebé
baby

el niño
child

el chico
boy

la chica
girl

la adolescente
teenager

el adulto
adult

el hombre
man

la mujer
woman

español • english

23

las relaciones • relationships

la ayudante	el jefe	la socia	el empleado	la empresaria	el compañero
assistant	manager	business partner	employee	employer	colleague

la oficina | office

el vecino
neighbour

el amigo
friend

el conocido
acquaintance

el amigo por correspondencia
penfriend

el novio
boyfriend

la novia
girlfriend

la pareja | couple

el prometido
fiancé

la prometida
fiancée

la pareja prometida | engaged couple

las emociones • emotions

la sonrisa
smile

contento
happy

triste
sad

entusiasmado
excited

aburrido
bored

sorprendido
surprised

asustado
scared

el ceño
fruncido
frown

enfadado
angry

confuso
confused

preocupado
worried

nervioso
nervous

orgulloso
proud

seguro de sí mismo
confident

avergonzado
embarrassed

tímido
shy

vocabulario • vocabulary

triste upset	**reír** laugh (v)	**suspirar** sigh (v)	**gritar** shout (v)
horrorizado shocked	**llorar** cry (v)	**desmayarse** faint (v)	**bostezar** yawn (v)

los acontecimientos de una vida • life events

nacer
be born (v)

empezar el colegio
start school (v)

hacer amigos
make friends (v)

licenciarse
graduate (v)

conseguir un trabajo
get a job (v)

enamorarse
fall in love (v)

casarse
get married (v)

tener un hijo
have a baby (v)

la boda | wedding

el divorcio
divorce

el funeral
funeral

vocabulario • vocabulary

el bautizo christening	**morir** die (v)
el bar mitzvah bar mitzvah	**hacer testamento** make a will (v)
el aniversario anniversary	**la partida de nacimiento** birth certificate
emigrar emigrate (v)	**la celebración de la boda** wedding reception
jubilarse retire (v)	**la luna de miel** honeymoon

las celebraciones • celebrations

la fiesta de cumpleaños
birthday party

la tarjeta
card

el regalo
present

el cumpleaños
birthday

la Navidad
Christmas

los festivales • festivals

la Pascua judía
Passover

el Año Nuevo
New Year

el carnaval
carnival

el desfile
procession

el Ramadán
Ramadan

el día de Acción de Gracias
Thanksgiving

la cinta
ribbon

la Semana Santa
Easter

el día de Halloween
Halloween

el Diwali
Diwali

el aspecto
appearance

la ropa de niño • children's clothing

el bebé • baby

el buzo
snowsuit

el body
vest

el corchete
popper

el pelele con pies
babygro

el pijama enterizo
sleepsuit

el pelele sin pies
romper suit

el babero
bib

las manoplas
mittens

los patucos
booties

el pañal de felpa
terry nappy

el pañal desechable
disposable nappy

braguitas de plástico
plastic pants

el niño pequeño • toddler

el gorro para el sol
sunhat

los panatalones con peto
dungarees

la camiseta
t-shirt

el delantal
apron

los pantalones cortos
shorts

la falda
skirt

el niño • child

el vestido
dress

los pantalones
vaqueros
jeans

la capucha
hood

las sandalias
sandals

el verano
summer

el impermeable
raincoat

la mochila
backpack

la muletilla
toggle

el otoño
autumn

la trenca
duffel coat

la bufanda
scarf

el chaquetón
anorak

las botas
de agua
wellington
boots

el invierno
winter

la bata
dressing gown

el logotipo
logo

las zapatillas
de deporte
trainers

el camisón
nightie

las zapatillas
slippers

la ropa para dormir
nightwear

el uniforme del
equipo
football strip

el chándal
tracksuit

las mallas
leggings

vocabulario • vocabulary

la fibra natural natural fibre	¿Se puede lavar a máquina? Is it machine washable?
sintético synthetic	¿Le valdrá esto a un niño de dos años? Will this fit a two-year-old?

la ropa de caballero • men's clothing

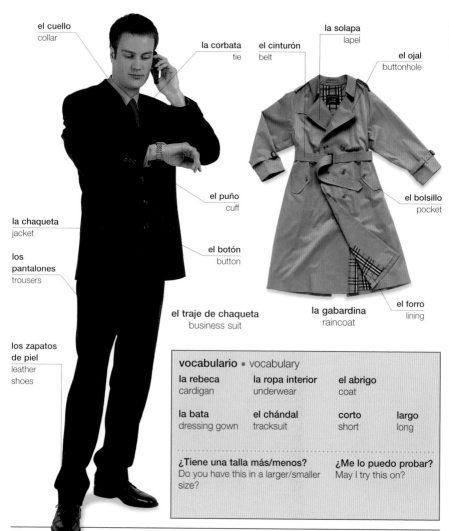

el cuello
collar

la corbata
tie

el cinturón
belt

la solapa
lapel

el ojal
buttonhole

el puño
cuff

el bolsillo
pocket

la chaqueta
jacket

los pantalones
trousers

el botón
button

el forro
lining

el traje de chaqueta
business suit

la gabardina
raincoat

los zapatos de piel
leather shoes

vocabulario • vocabulary

la rebeca cardigan	**la ropa interior** underwear	**el abrigo** coat
la bata dressing gown	**el chándal** tracksuit	**corto** short
		largo long

¿Tiene una talla más/menos?
Do you have this in a larger/smaller size?

¿Me lo puedo probar?
May I try this on?

la chaqueta
blazer

la americana sport
sports jacket

el chaleco
waistcoat

el cuello de pico
v-neck

el cuello
redondo
round neck

la camiseta
t-shirt

el chaquetón
anorak

la sudadera
sweatshirt

la camisa
shirt

los tejanos
jeans

el jersey
sweater

el pijama
pyjamas

la camiseta de tirantes
vest

la ropa casual
casual wear

los pantalones cortos
shorts

los calzoncillos
briefs

los calzoncillos de pata
boxer shorts

los calcetines
socks

la ropa de señora • women's clothing

la chaqueta
jacket

la costura
seam

la manga
sleeve

largo
ankle length

la falda
skirt

hasta la rodilla
knee-length

el dobladillo
hem

los zapatos
shoes

de vestir
formal

sin tirantes
strapless

sin mangas
sleeveless

el traje de noche
evening dress

el vestido
dress

la blusa
blouse

los pantalones
trousers

sport
casual

la lencería • lingerie

la bata
dressing gown

la combinación
slip

el tirante
strap

la camisola
camisole

las ligas
suspenders

el corsé con liguero
basque

la media
stocking

las medias
tights

el sujetador
bra

las bragas
knickers

el camisón
nightdress

la boda • wedding

el
encaje
lace

el velo
veil

el ramo de flores
bouquet

la cola
train

el vestido de novia
wedding dress

vocabulario • vocabulary	
el corsé corset	**sastre** tailored
la liga garter	**con aros** underwired
la hombrera shoulder pad	**la cinturilla** waistband
el sujetador deportivo sports bra	**al cuello y con los hombros al aire** halter neck

los accesorios • accessories

la gorra
cap

el sombrero
hat

el pañuelo
scarf

la hebilla
buckle

el cinturón
belt

el asa
handle

la punta
tip

el pañuelo
handkerchief

la pajarita
bow tie

el alfiler de corbata
tie-pin

los guantes
gloves

el paraguas
umbrella

las joyas • jewellery

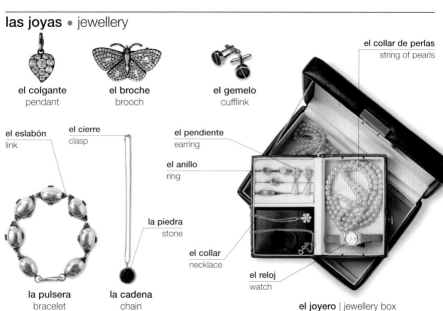

el colgante
pendant

el broche
brooch

el gemelo
cufflink

el collar de perlas
string of pearls

el eslabón
link

el cierre
clasp

el pendiente
earring

el anillo
ring

la piedra
stone

el collar
necklace

el reloj
watch

la pulsera
bracelet

la cadena
chain

el joyero | jewellery box

los bolsos • bags

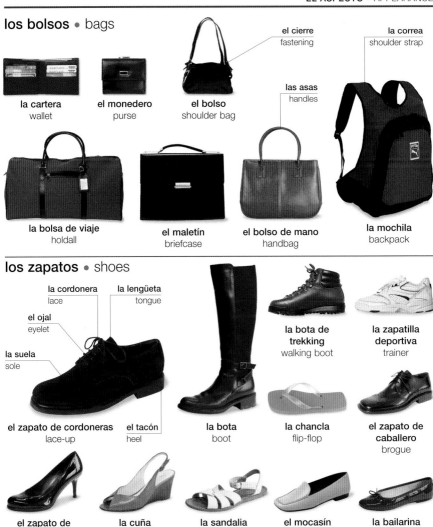

el cierre
fastening

la correa
shoulder strap

la cartera
wallet

el monedero
purse

el bolso
shoulder bag

las asas
handles

la bolsa de viaje
holdall

el maletín
briefcase

el bolso de mano
handbag

la mochila
backpack

los zapatos • shoes

la cordonera
lace

la lengüeta
tongue

el ojal
eyelet

la suela
sole

la bota de trekking
walking boot

la zapatilla deportiva
trainer

el zapato de cordoneras
lace-up

el tacón
heel

la bota
boot

la chancla
flip-flop

el zapato de caballero
brogue

el zapato de tacón
high heel shoe

la cuña
wedge

la sandalia
sandal

el mocasín
slip-on

la bailarina
pump

el pelo • hair

el peine
comb

peinar
comb (v)

el cepillo
brush

cepillar | brush (v)

la peluquera
hairdresser

el lavabo
sink

la clienta
client

lavar | wash (v)

enjuagar
rinse (v)

la bata
robe

cortar
cut (v)

secar con el secador
blow dry (v)

marcar
set (v)

los accesorios • accessories

el secador
hairdryer

el champú
shampoo

el suavizante
conditioner

el gel
gel

la laca
hairspray

las tenacillas
curling tongs

las tijeras
scissors

la diadema
hairband

la plancha de pelo
hair straighteners

la horquilla
hairpin

los estilos • styles

la cola de caballo	la trenza	el moño francés	el moño	las coletas
ponytail	plait	french pleat	bun	pigtails

la melena	el pelo corto	rizado	la permanente	lacio
bob	crop	curly	perm	straight

las raíces
roots

los reflejos	calvo	la peluca
highlights	bald	wig

los colores • colours

rubio	castaño	rojizo	pelirrojo
blonde	brunette	auburn	ginger

negro	gris	blanco	teñido
black	grey	white	dyed

vocabulario • vocabulary

la goma del pelo	graso
hairtie	greasy

| cortar las puntas | seco |
| trim (v) | dry |

| el barbero | normal |
| barber | normal |

| la caspa | alisar |
| dandruff | straighten (v) |

| las puntas abiertas | el cuero cabelludo |
| split ends | scalp |

la belleza • beauty

el tinte para el pelo
hair dye

la sombra
de ojos
eye shadow

el rímel
mascara

el lápiz de ojos
eyeliner

el colorete
blusher

el maquillaje de fondo
foundation

la barra de labios
lipstick

el maquillaje • make-up

el lápiz de cejas
eyebrow pencil

el cepillo para las cejas
eyebrow brush

las pinzas
tweezers

el brillo de labios
lip gloss

el pincel de labios
lip brush

el lápiz de labios
lip liner

la brocha
brush

el lápiz corrector
concealer

el espejo
mirror

los polvos
compactos
face powder

la borla
powder puff

la polvera | compact

los tratamientos de belleza •
beauty treatments

la mascarilla
face pack

la cama de rayos ultravioletas
sunbed

la limpieza de cutis
facial

exfoliar
exfoliate (v)

la depilación a la cera
wax

la pedicura
pedicure

los artículos de tocador •
toiletries

la leche limpiadora
cleanser

el tónico
toner

la crema hidratante
moisturizer

la crema auto-bronceadora
self-tanning cream

el perfume
perfume

el agua de colonia
eau de toilette

la manicura • manicure

el quitaesmalte
nail varnish remover

la lima de uñas
nail file

el esmalte de uñas
nail varnish

las tijeras de uñas
nail scissors

el cortaúñas
nail clippers

vocabulario • vocabulary

el cutis complexion	**graso** oily	**el bronceado** tan
claro fair	**sensible** sensitive	**el tatuaje** tattoo
moreno dark	**hipoalergénico** hypoallergenic	**antiarrugas** anti-wrinkle
seco dry	**el tono** shade	**las bolas de algodón** cotton balls

la salud
health

la enfermedad • illness

la fiebre | fever

el dolor de cabeza
headache

la hemorragia nasal
nosebleed

la tos
cough

el estornudo
sneeze

el resfriado
cold

la gripe
flu

el asma
asthma

el inhalador
inhaler

los calambres
cramps

la náusea
nausea

la varicela
chickenpox

el sarpullido
rash

vocabulario • vocabulary

el derrame cerebral stroke	la diabetes diabetes	el eccema eczema	el resfriado chill	vomitar vomit (v)	la diarrea diarrhoea
la tensión arterial blood pressure	la alergia allergy	el virus virus	la epilepsia epilepsy	desmayarse faint (v)	el sarampión measles
el infarto de miocardio heart attack	la fiebre del heno hayfever	la infección infection	el dolor de estómago stomach ache	la jaqueca migraine	las paperas mumps

el médico • doctor
la visita • consultation

la enfermera
nurse

el médico
doctor

el lector de rayos X
x-ray viewer

la receta
prescription

la paciente
patient

la báscula
scales

el monitor eléctrico
de la presión sanguínea
electric blood pressure monitor

el brazal
cuff

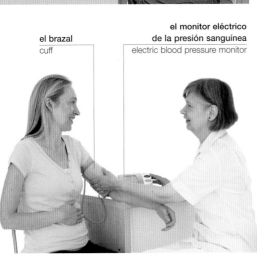

vocabulario • vocabulary

la cita	la inoculación
appointment	inoculation
la consulta	el termómetro
surgery	thermometer
la sala de	el examen
espera	médico
waiting room	medical
	examination

Necesito ver a un médico.
I need to see a doctor.

Me duele aquí.
It hurts here.

la lesión • injury

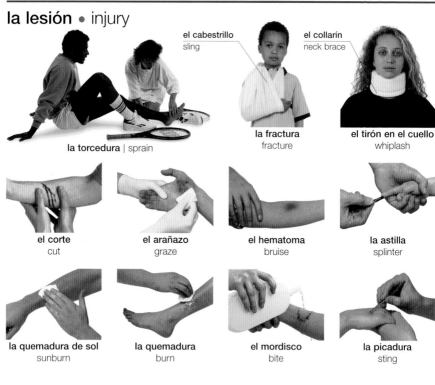

el cabestrillo
sling

el collarín
neck brace

la torcedura | sprain

la fractura
fracture

el tirón en el cuello
whiplash

el corte
cut

el arañazo
graze

el hematoma
bruise

la astilla
splinter

la quemadura de sol
sunburn

la quemadura
burn

el mordisco
bite

la picadura
sting

---

vocabulary • vocabulary

el accidente accident	**la hemorragia** haemorrhage	**la conmoción** concussion	**¿Se pondrá bien?** Will he/she be all right?
la urgencia emergency	**la ampolla** blister	**el envenenamiento** poisoning	**Por favor llame a una ambulancia.** Please call an ambulance.
la herida wound	**la lesión en la cabeza** head injury	**la descarga eléctrica** electric shock	**¿Dónde le duele?** Where does it hurt?

los primeros auxilios • first aid

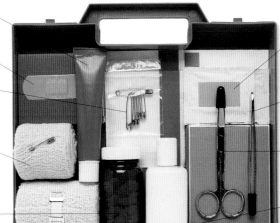

la pomada
ointment

la tirita
plaster

el imperdible
safety pin

la venda
bandage

los analgésicos
painkillers

la toallita antiséptica
antiseptic wipe

las pinzas
tweezers

las tijeras
scissors

el desinfectante
antiseptic

el botiquín | first aid box

la gasa
gauze

el vendaje
dressing

la tablilla
splint

el esparadrapo
adhesive tape

la reanimación
resuscitation

vocabulario • vocabulary			
el shock shock	**el pulso** pulse	**ahogarse** choke (v)	**¿Me puede ayudar?** Can you help?
inconsciente unconscious	**la respiración** breathing	**estéril** sterile	**¿Sabe primeros auxilios?** Do you know first aid?

el hospital • hospital

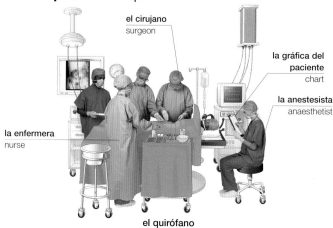

el cirujano
surgeon

la gráfica del
paciente
chart

la anestesista
anaesthetist

la enfermera
nurse

el quirófano
operating theatre

el análisis de sangre
blood test

la inyección
injection

la radiografía
x-ray

la camilla
trolley

el timbre
call button

la sala de urgencias
emergency room

la planta
ward

la silla de ruedas
wheelchair

la ecografía
scan

---

vocabulario • vocabulary

la operación operation	**dado de alta** discharged	**las horas de visita** visiting hours	**la sala de maternidad** maternity ward	**el paciente externo** outpatient
ingresado admitted	**la clínica** clinic	**la sala de pediatría** children's ward	**la habitación privada** private room	**la unidad de** **cuidados intensivos** intensive care unit

los servicios • departments

la otorrinonaringología
ENT

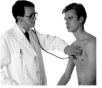

la cardiología
cardiology

la ortopedia
orthopaedy

la ginecología
gynaecology

la fisioterapia
physiotherapy

la dermatología
dermatology

la pediatría
paediatrics

la radiología
radiology

la cirugía
surgery

la maternidad
maternity

la psiquiatría
psychiatry

la oftalmología
ophthalmology

---

vocabulario • vocabulary

la neurología neurology	**la urología** urology	**la cirugía plástica** plastic surgery	**la patología** pathology	**el resultado** result
la oncología oncology	**la endocrinología** endocrinology	**el volante** referral	**el análisis** test	**el especialista** consultant

---

el dentista • dentist

el diente • tooth

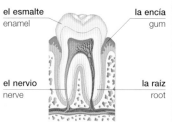

el esmalte
enamel

la encía
gum

el nervio
nerve

la raíz
root

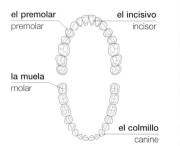

el premolar
premolar

el incisivo
incisor

la muela
molar

el colmillo
canine

---

vocabulario • vocabulary

el dolor de muelas
toothache

el hilo dental
dental floss

la placa bacteriana
plaque

la extracción
extraction

la caries
decay

la corona
crown

el empaste
filling

el torno del dentista
drill

la revisión • check-up

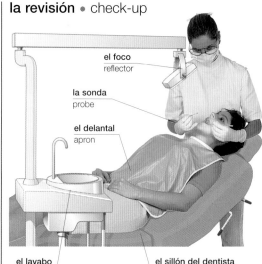

el foco
reflector

la sonda
probe

el delantal
apron

el lavabo
basin

el sillón del dentista
dentist's chair

usar el hilo
dental
floss (v)

cepillarse los
dientes
brush (v)

el aparato
corrector
brace

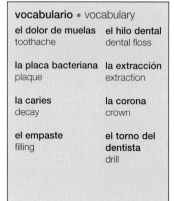

los rayos x
dentales
dental x-ray

la radiografía
x-ray film

la dentadura
postiza
dentures

el óptico · optician

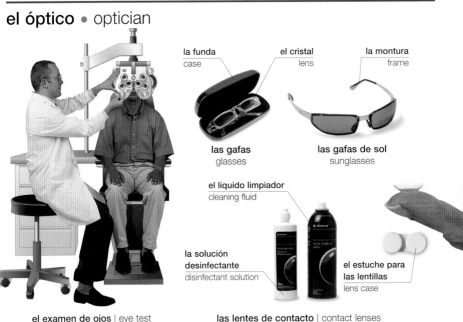

la funda
case

el cristal
lens

la montura
frame

las gafas
glasses

las gafas de sol
sunglasses

el líquido limpiador
cleaning fluid

la solución
desinfectante
disinfectant solution

el estuche para
las lentillas
lens case

el examen de ojos | eye test

las lentes de contacto | contact lenses

el ojo · eye

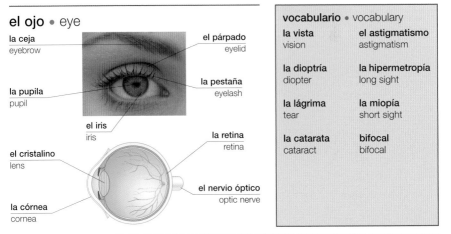

la ceja
eyebrow

el párpado
eyelid

la pupila
pupil

la pestaña
eyelash

el iris
iris

el cristalino
lens

la retina
retina

la córnea
cornea

el nervio óptico
optic nerve

vocabulario · vocabulary	
la vista vision	**el astigmatismo** astigmatism
la dioptría diopter	**la hipermetropía** long sight
la lágrima tear	**la miopía** short sight
la catarata cataract	**bifocal** bifocal

el embarazo • pregnancy

la enfermera
nurse

la prueba del embarazo
pregnancy test

el cordón
umbilical
umbilical cord

la placenta
placenta

el cuello uterino
cervix

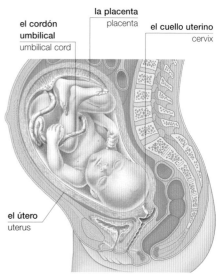

la ecografía
scan

el útero
uterus

el ultrasonido | ultrasound

el feto | foetus

---

vocabulario • vocabulary

la ovulación ovulation	**prenatal** antenatal	**la contracción** contraction	**la dilatación** dilation	**los puntos** stitches	**de nalgas** breech
la concepción conception	**el trimestre** trimester	**romper aguas** break waters (v)	**la epidural** epidural	**el parto** delivery	**prematuro** premature
embarazada pregnant	**el embrión** embryo	**la amniocentesis** amniocentesis	**la episiotomía** episiotomy	**el nacimiento** birth	**el ginecólogo** gynaecologist
encinta expectant	**la matriz** womb	**el líquido amniótico** amniotic fluid	**la cesárea** caesarean section	**el aborto espontáneo** miscarriage	**el tocólogo** obstetrician

el parto • childbirth

el gotero
drip

la comadrona
midwife

el monitor
monitor

el catéter
catheter

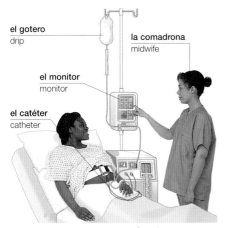

provocar el parto
induce labour (v)

la incubadora | incubator

la báscula
scales

el peso al nacer | birth weight

los fórceps
forceps

la ventosa
ventouse cup

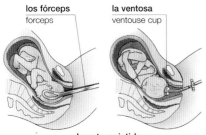

el parto asistido
assisted delivery

la pulsera de identificación
identity tag

el recién nacido
newborn baby

la lactancia • nursing

el sacaleches
breast pump

**el sujetador para la
lactancia**
nursing bra

dar el pecho
breastfeed (v)

los discos protectores
pads

las terapias alternativas • alternative therapy

la camiseta
t-shirt

la colchoneta
mat

el yoga | yoga

el masaje
massage

el shiatsu
shiatsu

la quiropráctica
chiropractic

la osteopatía
osteopathy

la reflexología
reflexology

la meditación
meditation

el terapeuta
counsellor

la terapia de grupo
group therapy

el reiki
reiki

la acupuntura
acupuncture

la ayurveda
ayurveda

la hipnoterapia
hypnotherapy

los aceites esenciales
essential oils

el herbolario
herbalism

la aromaterapia
aromatherapy

la homeopatía
homeopathy

la acupresión
acupressure

la terapeuta
therapist

la psicoterapia
psychotherapy

vocabulario • vocabulary

la cristaloterapia crystal healing	**la naturopatía** naturopathy	**la relajación** relaxation	**la hierba** herb
la hidroterapia hydrotherapy	**el feng shui** feng shui	**el estrés** stress	**el suplemento** supplement

la casa
home

la casa • house

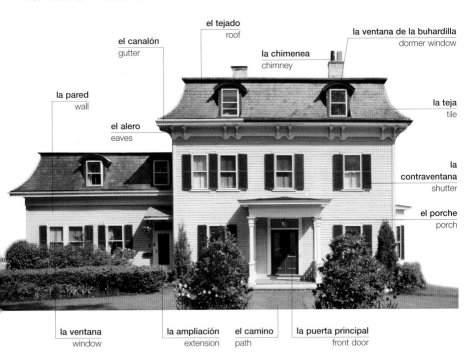

el tejado
roof

el canalón
gutter

la chimenea
chimney

la ventana de la buhardilla
dormer window

la pared
wall

el alero
eaves

la teja
tile

la contraventana
shutter

el porche
porch

la ventana
window

la ampliación
extension

el camino
path

la puerta principal
front door

vocabulario • vocabulary

adosado terraced	**el sótano** basement	**el garaje** garage	**el piso** floor	**el buzón** letterbox	**alquilar** rent (v)
no adosado detached	**la vivienda urbana** townhouse	**el ático** attic	**el patio** courtyard	**el propietario** landlord	**el alquiler** rent
adosado por un lado semidetached	**la vivienda de una planta** bungalow	**la habitación** room	**la luz del porche** porch light	**la alarma antirrobo** burglar alarm	**el inquilino** tenant

la entrada • entrance

el piso • flat

el pasamanos
hand rail

el descansillo
landing

la barandilla
banister

la escalera
staircase

el vestíbulo
hallway

el timbre
doorbell

el felpudo
doormat

la aldaba
door knocker

la cadena
door chain

la llave
key

la cerradura
lock

el cerrojo
bolt

el balcón
balcony

el edificio
block of flats

el interfono
intercom

el ascensor
lift

las instalaciones internas • internal systems

la hoja
blade

ventilador
fan

el radiador
radiator

la estufa
heater

el calentador de
convección
convector heater

la electricidad • electricity

el filamento
filament

la toma de tierra
earthing

la clavija
pin

neutro
neutral

con corriente
live

la bombilla de ahorro de energía
energy-saving bulb

el enchufe macho
plug

los cables
wires

---

vocabulario • vocabulary

el voltaje voltage	el generador generator	el enchufe hembra socket	la corriente continua direct current	el transformador transformer
el amperio amp	el fusible fuse	el interruptor switch	el contador de la luz electricity meter	el suministro de electricidad mains supply
la corriente eléctrica power	la caja de los fusibles fuse box	la corriente alterna alternating current	el corte de luz power cut	

---

español • english

la fontanería • plumbing

la toma
inlet

la salida
outlet

la válvula
de la
presión
pressure
valve

el
aislamiento
insulation

el tubo de
desagüe
overflow
pipe

el tanque
tank

el tanque
del agua
water
chamber

la llave
del
desagüe
drain cock

el termostato
thermostat

el quemador
gas burner

la resistencia
heating element

la caldera
boiler

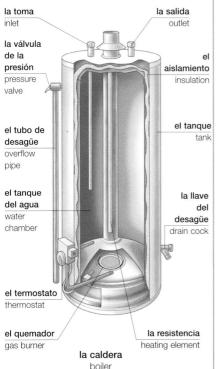

el fregador • sink

el grifo
tap

la palanca
lever

la toma
del agua
supply pipe

la junta
gasket

la llave de paso
shutoff valve

el desagüe
drain

el triturador de basuras
waste disposal unit

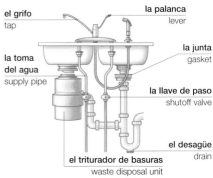

el retrete • water closet

la cisterna
cistern

el flotador
float ball

la tapa
seat

la taza
bowl

el desagüe
waste pipe

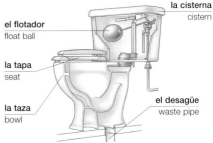

la eliminación de desechos • waste disposal

la botella
bottle

la tapa
lid

el pedal
pedal

el cubo para
reciclar
recycling bin

el cubo de
la basura
rubbish bin

el armario para
clasificar la basura
sorting unit

los despercicios
orgánicos
organic waste

el cuarto de estar • living room

el aplique
wall light

la cheminée
fireplace

el techo
ceiling

le vase
vase

el cojín
cushion

la lámpara
lamp

**la mesa
de café**
coffee table

el sofá
sofa

el suelo
floor

el marco
frame

el cuadro
painting

la cortina
curtain

el visillo
net curtain

el estor de láminas
venetian blind

el estor
roller blind

la moldura
moulding

el sillón
armchair

la estantería
bookshelf

el sofá-cama
sofabed

la alfombra
rug

el despacho | study

el comedor • dining room

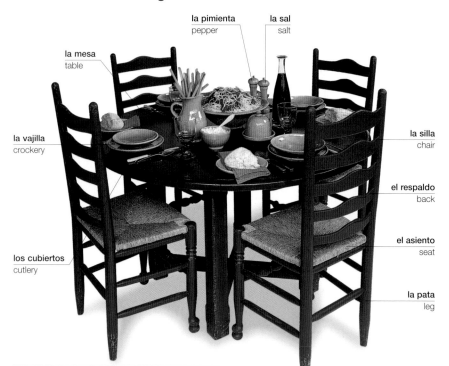

la pimienta
pepper

la sal
salt

la mesa
table

la vajilla
crockery

la silla
chair

el respaldo
back

el asiento
seat

los cubiertos
cutlery

la pata
leg

vocabulario • vocabulary

servir serve (v)	**la comida** meal	**el desayuno** breakfast	**hambriento** hungry	**el anfitrión** host	**Estaba buenísimo.** That was delicious.
comer eat (v)	**el mantel** tablecloth	**la comida** lunch	**lleno** full	**la anfitriona** hostess	**Estoy lleno, gracias.** I've had enough, thank you.
poner la mesa lay the table (v)	**el mantel individual** place mat	**la cena** dinner	**la ración** portion	**el invitado** guest	**¿Puedo repetir, por favor?** Can I have some more, please?

la vajilla y los cubiertos • crockery and cutlery

la cucharilla de café
teaspoon

la taza
mug

la taza de café
coffee cup

la taza de té
teacup

el plato
plate

el bol
bowl

la copa de vino
wine glass

el vaso
tumbler

**la cafetera
de émbolo**
cafetière

la tetera
teapot

la jarra
jug

la huevera
egg cup

la cristalería
glassware

el plato del pan
side plate

el plato llano
dinner plate

**el plato
sopero**
soup bowl

la cuchara sopera
soup spoon

el servilletero
napkin ring

el tenedor
fork

la cuchara
spoon

el cuchillo
knife

la servilleta
napkin

el cubierto
place setting

la cocina • kitchen

los estantes
shelves

el frente de la
cocina
splashback

el grifo
tap

el fregadero
sink

el cajón
drawer

el extractor
extractor

la placa vitro-
cerámica
ceramic hob

la encimera
worktop

el horno
oven

el armario
cabinet

los electrodomésticos • appliances

el cuenco
mezclador
mixing bowl

la tapa
lid

el horno microondas
microwave oven

la cuchilla
blade

el hervidor
kettle

el tostador
toaster

el robot de cocina
food processor

la licuadora
blender

el friegaplatos
dishwasher

la máquina de los cubitos
ice maker

el frigorífico
refrigerator

el estante
shelf

el congelador
freezer

el cajón de
las verduras
crisper

el frigorífico congelador | fridge-freezer

vocabulario • vocabulary

la placa hob	**congelar** freeze (v)
el escurridor draining board	**descongelar** defrost (v)
el quemador burner	**saltear** sauté (v)
el cubo de basura rubbish bin	**cocer al vapor** steam (v)

cocinar • cooking

pelar
peel (v)

cortar
slice (v)

rallar
grate (v)

echar
pour (v)

mezclar
mix (v)

batir
whisk (v)

hervir
boil (v)

freír
fry (v)

extender con el rodillo
roll (v)

remover
stir (v)

cocer a fuego lento
simmer (v)

escalfar
poach (v)

cocer al horno
bake (v)

asar
roast (v)

asar a la parrilla
grill (v)

los utensilios de cocina • kitchenware

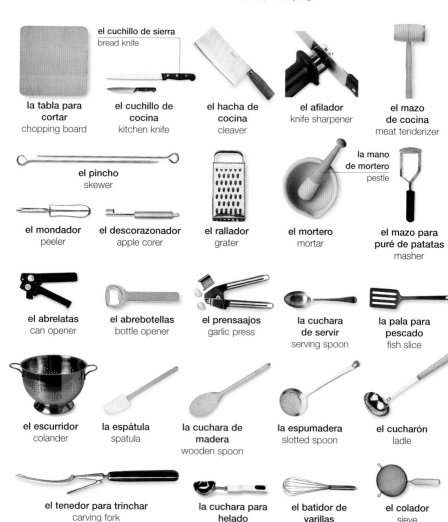

el cuchillo de sierra
bread knife

la tabla para cortar
chopping board

el cuchillo de cocina
kitchen knife

el hacha de cocina
cleaver

el afilador
knife sharpener

el mazo de cocina
meat tenderizer

el pincho
skewer

la mano de mortero
pestle

el mondador
peeler

el descorazonador
apple corer

el rallador
grater

el mortero
mortar

el mazo para puré de patatas
masher

el abrelatas
can opener

el abrebotellas
bottle opener

el prensaajos
garlic press

la cuchara de servir
serving spoon

la pala para pescado
fish slice

el escurridor
colander

la espátula
spatula

la cuchara de madera
wooden spoon

la espumadera
slotted spoon

el cucharón
ladle

el tenedor para trinchar
carving fork

la cuchara para helado
scoop

el batidor de varillas
whisk

el colador
sieve

la tapa
lid

antiadherente
non-stick

la sartén
frying pan

el cazo
saucepan

la parrilla
grill pan

el wok
wok

**la cazuela de
barro**
earthenware dish

de cristal
glass

resistente al horno
ovenproof

el cuenco
mixing bowl

el molde para suflé
soufflé dish

**la fuente para
gratinar**
gratin dish

**el molde
individual**
ramekin

la cazuela
casserole dish

la repostería • baking cakes

**la báscula de
cocina**
scales

**la jarra
graduada**
measuring jug

**el molde para
bizcocho**
cake tin

el molde redondo
pie tin

la flanera
flan tin

la brocha de cocina
pastry brush

el rodillo de cocina
rolling pin

la manga pastelera
piping bag

**el molde para
magdalenas**
muffin tray

**la bandeja de
horno**
baking tray

la rejilla
cooling rack

**la manopla de
cocina**
oven glove

el delantal
apron

el dormitorio • bedroom

el armario
wardrobe

**la lámpara de
la mesilla**
bedside lamp

el cabecero
headboard

la mesilla de noche
bedside table

la cómoda
chest of drawers

el cajón
drawer

la cama
bed

el colchón
mattress

la colcha
bedspread

la almohada
pillow

**la bolsa de
agua caliente**
hot-water bottle

**la radio
despertador**
clock radio

**el reloj
despertador**
alarm clock

**la caja de pañuelos
de papel**
box of tissues

la percha
coat hanger

la ropa de cama • bed linen

el espejo
mirror

el tocador
dressing
table

el suelo
floor

la funda de la
almohada
pillowcase

la sábana
sheet

el cubrecanapé
valance

el edredón
duvet

la colcha
quilt

la manta
blanket

vocabulario • vocabulary

la cama individual single bed	**el estribo** footboard	**el insomnio** insomnia	**despertarse** wake up (v)	**roncar** snore (v)
la manta eléctrica electric blanket	**el muelle** spring	**acostarse** go to bed (v)	**levantarse** get up (v)	**hacer la cama** make the bed (v)
la cama de matrimonio double bed	**la moqueta** carpet	**dormirse** go to sleep (v)	**poner el despertador** set the alarm (v)	**el armario empotrado** built-in wardrobe

el cuarto de baño • bathroom

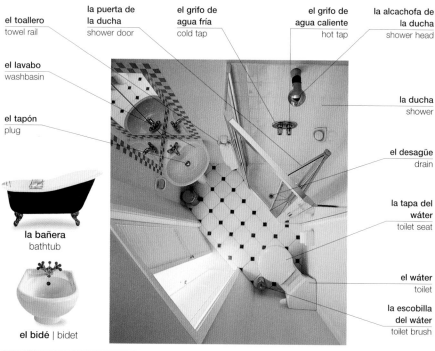

el toallero
towel rail

la puerta de la ducha
shower door

el grifo de agua fría
cold tap

el grifo de agua caliente
hot tap

la alcachofa de la ducha
shower head

el lavabo
washbasin

la ducha
shower

el tapón
plug

el desagüe
drain

la bañera
bathtub

la tapa del wáter
toilet seat

el bidé | bidet

el wáter
toilet

la escobilla del wáter
toilet brush

---

vocabulario • vocabulary

el armario de las medicinas
medicine cabinet

la alfombrilla de baño
bath mat

el rollo de papel higiénico
toilet roll

la cortina de ducha
shower curtain

darse una ducha
take a shower (v)

darse un baño
take a bath (v)

la higiene dental • dental hygiene

el cepillo de dientes
toothbrush

la pasta de dientes
toothpaste

el hilo dental
dental floss

el enjuague bucal
mouthwash

la esponja
sponge

la piedra pómez
pumice stone

el cepillo para la
espalda
back brush

el desodorante
deodorant

la jabonera
soap dish

el gel de ducha
shower gel

el jabón
soap

la crema para la cara
face cream

el gel de baño
bubble bath

la toalla de
lavabo
hand towel

la toalla de
baño
bath towel

las toallas
towels

la leche del cuerpo
body lotion

los polvos de talco
talcum powder

el albornoz
bathrobe

el afeitado • shaving

la maquinilla
eléctrica
electric razor

la espuma de afeitar
shaving foam

la hoja de
afeitar
razor blade

la cuchilla de
afeitar desechable
disposable razor

el aftershave
aftershave

la habitación de los niños • nursery

el cuidado del bebé • baby care

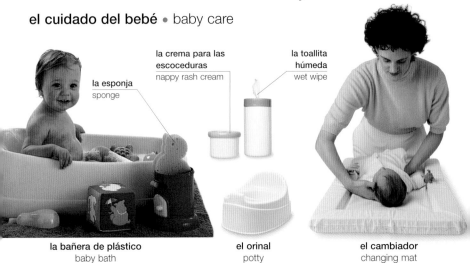

la crema para las escoceduras
nappy rash cream

la toallita húmeda
wet wipe

la esponja
sponge

la bañera de plástico
baby bath

el orinal
potty

el cambiador
changing mat

la hora de dormir • sleeping

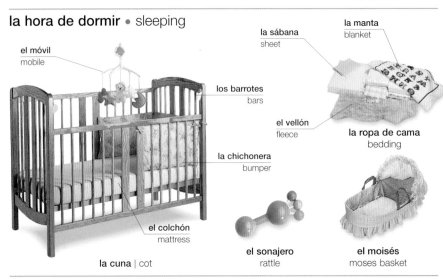

la sábana
sheet

la manta
blanket

el móvil
mobile

los barrotes
bars

el vellón
fleece

la ropa de cama
bedding

la chichonera
bumper

el colchón
mattress

la cuna | cot

el sonajero
rattle

el moisés
moses basket

los juegos • playing

la muñeca
doll

el muñeco de peluche
soft toy

la casa de muñecas
doll's house

la casa de juguetes
playhouse

el oso de peluche
teddy bear

el juguete
toy

el cesto de los juguetes
toy basket

la pelota
ball

el parque
playpen

la seguridad • safety

el cierre de seguridad
child lock

el escuchabebés
baby monitor

la barrera de seguridad
stair gate

la comida • eating

la trona
high chair

la tetina
teat

la taza
drinking cup

el biberón
bottle

el paseo • going out

la silleta de paseo
pushchair

el cochecito de niños
pram

la capota
hood

el capazo
carrycot

el pañal
nappy

la bolsa del bebé
changing bag

la mochila de bebé
baby sling

el lavadero • utility room

la colada • laundry

la ropa limpia
clean clothes

la ropa sucia
dirty washing

el cesto de la
colada
laundry basket

la lavadora
washing machine

la lavadora
secadora
washer-dryer

la secadora
tumble dryer

el cesto de la
ropa de plancha
linen basket

la cuerda para
tender la ropa
clothes line

la plancha
iron

la pinza para la
ropa
clothes peg

secar
dry (v)

la tabla de la plancha | ironing board

---

vocabulario • vocabulary

cargar	centrifugar	planchar	¿Cómo funciona la lavadora?
load (v)	spin (v)	iron (v)	How do I operate the washing machine?
aclarar	la centrifugadora	el suavizante	¿Cuál es el programa para la ropa de
rinse (v)	spin dryer	fabric conditioner	color/blanca?
			What is the setting for coloureds/whites?

---

español • english

el equipo de limpieza • cleaning equipment

el tubo de la aspiradora
suction hose

el cepillo
brush

el recogedor
dust pan

la lejía
bleach

el cubo
bucket

en polvo
powder

líquido
liquid

el trapo del polvo
duster

la aspiradora
vacuum cleaner

la fregona
mop

el detergente
detergent

la cera
polish

las acciones • activities

limpiar
clean (v)

fregar
wash (v)

pasar la bayeta
wipe (v)

restregar
scrub (v)

raspar
scrape (v)

la escoba
broom

barrer
sweep (v)

limpiar el polvo
dust (v)

sacar brillo
polish (v)

el taller • workshop

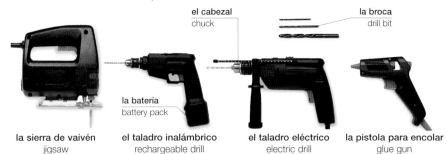

el cabezal
chuck

la broca
drill bit

la batería
battery pack

la sierra de vaivén
jigsaw

el taladro inalámbrico
rechargeable drill

el taladro eléctrico
electric drill

la pistola para encolar
glue gun

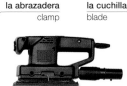

la abrazadera
clamp

la cuchilla
blade

el torno de banco
vice

la lijadora
sander

la sierra circular
circular saw

el banco de trabajo
workbench

la cola de carpintero
wood glue

el organizador de
las herramientas
tool rack

la guimbarda
router

el taladro manual
bit brace

las virutas de madera
wood shavings

el alargador
extension lead

las técnicas • techniques

cortar
cut (v)

serrar
saw (v)

taladrar
drill (v)

clavar con el martillo
hammer (v)

alisar
plane (v)

tornear
turn (v)

el hilo de estaño
solder

tallar
carve (v)

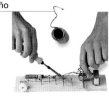
soldar
solder (v)

los materiales • materials

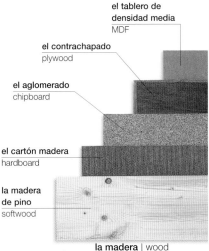

el tablero de
densidad media
MDF

el contrachapado
plywood

el aglomerado
chipboard

el cartón madera
hardboard

la madera
de pino
softwood

la madera | wood

la madera noble
hardwood

el barniz
varnish

el tinte para
madera
woodstain

el alambre
wire

el cable
cable

el acero inoxidable
stainless steel

galvanizado
galvanised

el metal | metal

la caja de las herramientas • toolbox

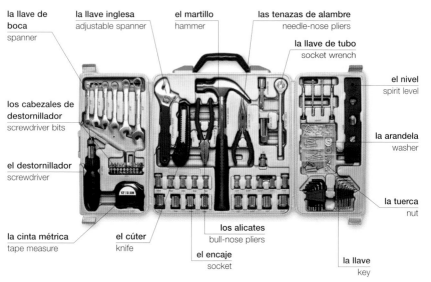

la llave de boca
spanner

la llave inglesa
adjustable spanner

el martillo
hammer

las tenazas de alambre
needle-nose pliers

la llave de tubo
socket wrench

los cabezales de destornillador
screwdriver bits

el nivel
spirit level

el destornillador
screwdriver

la arandela
washer

la tuerca
nut

la cinta métrica
tape measure

el cúter
knife

los alicates
bull-nose pliers

el encaje
socket

la llave
key

las brocas • drill bits

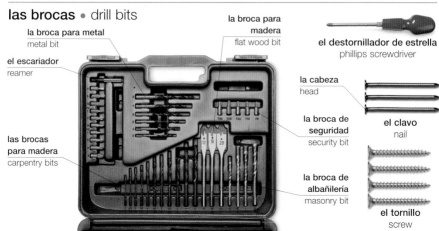

la broca para metal
metal bit

la broca para madera
flat wood bit

el escariador
reamer

el destornillador de estrella
phillips screwdriver

la cabeza
head

las brocas para madera
carpentry bits

la broca de seguridad
security bit

el clavo
nail

la broca de albañilería
masonry bit

el tornillo
screw

el pelacables
wire strippers

el cortaalambres
wire cutters

el soldador
soldering iron

la cinta
aislante
insulating
tape

la sierra de calar
fretsaw

el hilo de
estaño
solder

el escalpelo
scalpel

el serrucho de costilla | tenon saw

las gafas de
seguridad
safety goggles

el cepillo
plane

el serrucho
handsaw

la caja para cortar
en inglete
mitre block

la sierra para metales
hacksaw

el taladro manual
hand drill

la lana de acero
wire wool

las tenazas
wrench

el formón
chisel

el papel de lija
sandpaper

el desatascador
plunger

la lima
file

la piedra
afiladora
sharpening stone

el cortatuberías | pipe cutter

la decoración • decorating

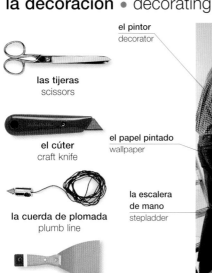

el pintor
decorator

la brocha de empapelador
wallpaper brush

las tijeras
scissors

el cúter
craft knife

el papel pintado
wallpaper

la mesa de encolar
pasting table

la brocha de encolar
pasting brush

la cuerda de plomada
plumb line

la escalera de mano
stepladder

la cola para empapelar
wallpaper paste

el cubo
bucket

el raspador
scraper

empapelar | wallpaper (v)

arrancar
strip (v)

rellenar
fill (v)

lijar
sand (v)

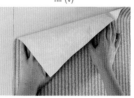

enyesar | plaster (v)

empapelar | hang (v)

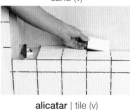

alicatar | tile (v)

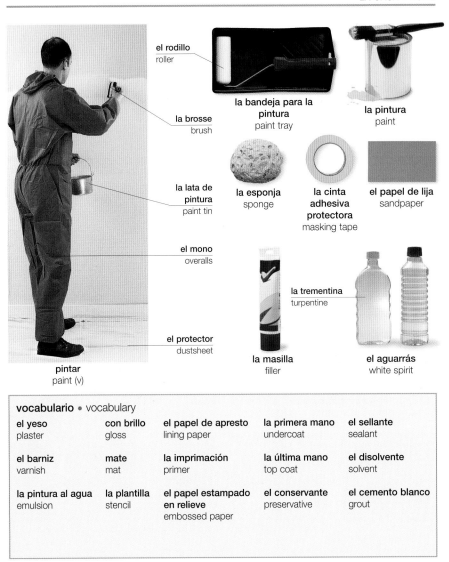

el rodillo
roller

la bandeja para la pintura
paint tray

la pintura
paint

la brosse
brush

la esponja
sponge

la cinta adhesiva protectora
masking tape

el papel de lija
sandpaper

la lata de pintura
paint tin

el mono
overalls

la trementina
turpentine

el protector
dustsheet

la masilla
filler

el aguarrás
white spirit

pintar
paint (v)

vocabulario • vocabulary

el yeso plaster	**con brillo** gloss	**el papel de apresto** lining paper	**la primera mano** undercoat	**el sellante** sealant
el barniz varnish	**mate** mat	**la imprimación** primer	**la última mano** top coat	**el disolvente** solvent
la pintura al agua emulsion	**la plantilla** stencil	**el papel estampado en relieve** embossed paper	**el conservante** preservative	**el cemento blanco** grout

el jardín • garden

los estilos de jardín • garden styles

la terraza ajardinada
patio garden

el jardín en la azotea
roof garden

los adornos para el jardín • garden features

la cesta colgante
hanging basket

la rocalla
rock garden

la espaldera
trellis

el jardín clásico | formal garden

el patio
courtyard

el jardín campestre
cottage garden

el jardín de plantas herbáceas
herb garden

el jardín acuático
water garden

la pérgola
pergola

el montón de abono compuesto
compost heap

la terraza
paving

el camino
path

la puerta
gate

el parterre
flowerbed

la tierra • soil

la capa superior
de la tierra
topsoil

la arena
sand

el cobertizo
shed

el invernadero
greenhouse

el césped
lawn

la creta
chalk

el estanque
pond

la valla
fence

el seto
hedge

el arco
arch

el huerto
vegetable
garden

el arriate de plantas
herbáceas
herbaceous border

el cieno
silt

el entarimado
decking

la fuente | fountain

la arcilla
clay

las plantas de jardín • garden plants

los tipos de plantas • types of plants

anual
annual

bienal
biennial

perenne
perennial

el bulbo
bulb

el helecho
fern

el junco
rush

el bambú
bamboo

las malas hierbas
weeds

la hierba
herb

la planta acuática
water plant

el árbol
tree

la palmera
palm

la conífera
conifer

de hoja perenne
evergreen

de hoja caduca
deciduous

**las plantas podadas
con formas**
topiary

la planta alpestre
alpine

la planta suculenta
succulent

el cactus
cactus

la planta de maceta
potted plant

la planta de sombra
shade plant

**la planta
trepadora**
climber

**el arbusto
de flor**
flowering shrub

**la planta para
cubrir suelo**
ground cover

la planta trepadora
creeper

ornamental
ornamental

el césped
grass

las herramientas de jardinería • garden tools

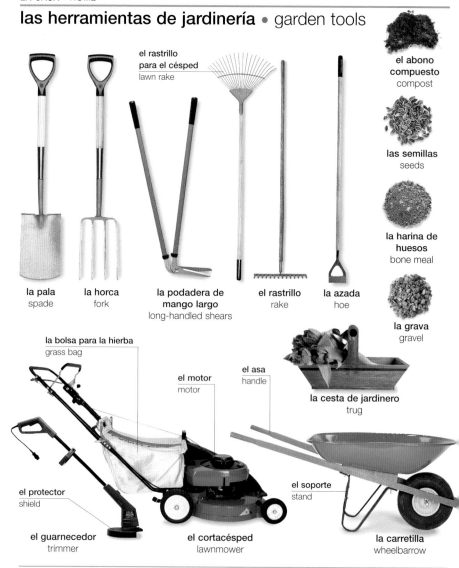

el abono
compuesto
compost

las semillas
seeds

la harina de
huesos
bone meal

la grava
gravel

el rastrillo
para el césped
lawn rake

la pala
spade

la horca
fork

la podadera de
mango largo
long-handled shears

el rastrillo
rake

la azada
hoe

la bolsa para la hierba
grass bag

el motor
motor

el asa
handle

la cesta de jardinero
trug

el protector
shield

el soporte
stand

el guarnecedor
trimmer

el cortacésped
lawnmower

la carretilla
wheelbarrow

la horquilla
hand fork

las tijeras de podar
secateurs

los guantes de jardín
gardening gloves

el desplantador
trowel

el hilo de bramante
twine

las etiquetas
labels

la hoja
blade

el semillero
seed tray

el alambre
twist ties

las anillas
ring ties

la cizalla
shears

las cañas
canes

la criba
sieve

el pesticida
pesticide

la maceta
plant pot

la sierra de mano
hand saw

las botas de goma
rubber boots

el riego • watering

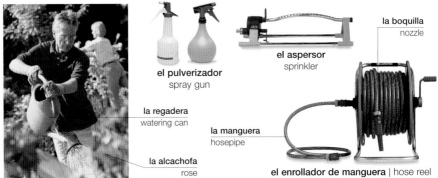

el pulverizador
spray gun

el aspersor
sprinkler

la boquilla
nozzle

la regadera
watering can

la manguera
hosepipe

la alcachofa
rose

el enrollador de manguera | hose reel

la jardinería • gardening

el césped
lawn

el parterre
flowerbed

el cortacésped
lawnmower

el seto
hedge

la estaca
stake

cortar el césped | mow (v)

poner césped
turf (v)

hacer agujeros con la horquilla
spike (v)

rastrillar
rake (v)

podar
trim (v)

cavar
dig (v)

sembrar
sow (v)

abonar en la superficie
top dress (v)

regar
water (v)

la caña
cane

guiar
train (v)

quitar las flores muertas
deadhead (v)

rociar
spray (v)

injertar
graft (v)

el esqueje
cutting
propagar
propagate (v)

podar
prune (v)

apuntalar
stake (v)

transplantar
transplant (v)

escardar
weed (v)

cubrir la tierra
mulch (v)

cosechar
harvest (v)

vocabulario • vocabulary

cultivar cultivate (v)	**diseñar** landscape (v)	**abonar** fertilize (v)	**cribar** sieve (v)	**biológico** organic	**el plantón** seedling	**el subsuelo** subsoil
cuidar tend (v)	**plantar en tiesto** pot up (v)	**coger** pick (v)	**airear** aerate (v)	**el drenaje** drainage	**el abono** fertilizer	**el herbicida** weedkiller

los servicios
services

los servicios de emergencia • emergency services

la ambulancia • ambulance

la ambulancia
ambulance

la camilla
stretcher

el ambulancero
paramedic

la policía • police

las luces
lights

el uniforme
uniform

la sirena
siren

la placa
badge

el coche de policía
police car

la estación de policía
police station

la porra
truncheon

la pistola
gun

las esposas
handcuffs

el agente de policía
police officer

vocabulario • vocabulary

el comisario inspector	el robo burglary	la denuncia complaint	el arresto arrest
el detective detective	la agresión assault	la investigación investigation	la celda police cell
el crimen crime	la huella **dactilar** fingerprint	el sospechoso suspect	el cargo charge

los bomberos • fire brigade

el casco
helmet

el humo
smoke

la manguera
hose

la cesta
cradle

el chorro de agua
water jet

los bomberos
fire fighters

la cabina
cab

el brazo
boom

la escalera
ladder

el incendio | fire

el parque de bomberos
fire station

la salida de incendios
fire escape

el coche de bomberos
fire engine

el detector de humos
smoke alarm

la alarma contra incendios
fire alarm

el hacha
axe

el extintor
fire extinguisher

la boca de agua
hydrant

Necesito la policía/los bomberos/una ambulancia. I need the police/fire brigade/ambulance.	**Hay un incendio en…** There's a fire at…	**Ha habido un accidente.** There's been an accident.	**¡Llame a la policía!** Call the police!

el banco • bank

el cliente — customer
la ventanilla — window
el cajero — cashier
los folletos — leaflets
el mostrador — counter
las hojas de ingreso — paying-in slips

la tarjeta de débito — debit card
la matriz — stub
el número de cuenta — account number
la firma — signature
la cantidad — amount

el director de banco — bank manager
la tarjeta de crédito — credit card
el talonario de cheques — chequebook
el cheque — cheque

vocabulario • vocabulary

los ahorros — savings	la hipoteca — mortgage	el pago — payment	ingresar — pay in (v)	la cuenta corriente — current account
los impuestos — tax	el descubierto — overdraft	la hoja de reintegro — withdrawal slip	el pin — pin number	la cuenta de ahorros — savings account
el préstamo — loan	el tipo de interés — interest rate	la domiciliación bancaria — direct debit	a transferencia bancaria — bank transfer	la comisión bancaria — bank charge

la moneda
coin

el billete
note

la pantalla
screen

el teclado
key pad

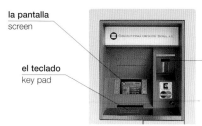

la ranura de
la tarjeta
card slot

el dinero
money

el cajero automático
cash machine

las divisas • foreign currency

la oficina de cambio
bureau de change

el cheque de viaje
traveller's cheque

el tipo de
cambio
exchange rate

las finanzas • finance

el valor de las
acciones
share price

el agente de
bolsa
stockbroker

la asesora financiera
financial advisor

la bolsa de valores | stock exchange

vocabulario • vocabulary

cobrar
cash (v)

las acciones
shares

el valor nominal
denomination

los dividendos
dividends

la comisión
commission

el contable
accountant

la inversión
investment

la cartera
portfolio

las acciones
stocks

el patrimonio neto
equity

¿Podría cambiar esto por favor?
Can I change this please?

¿A cuánto está el cambio hoy?
What's today's exchange rate?

las comunicaciones • communications

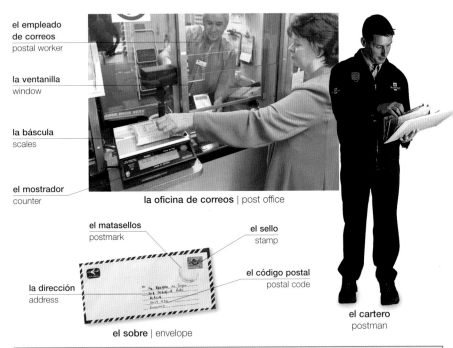

el empleado
de correos
postal worker

la ventanilla
window

la báscula
scales

el mostrador
counter

la oficina de correos | post office

el matasellos
postmark

el sello
stamp

el código postal
postal code

la dirección
address

el sobre | envelope

el cartero
postman

vocabulario • vocabulary

la carta letter	**el remite** return address	**el reparto** delivery	**frágil** fragile	**no doblar** do not bend (v)
por avión by airmail	**la firma** signature	**el franqueo** postage	**la saca postal** mailbag	**hacia arriba** this way up
el correo cer- **tificado** registered post	**la recogida** collection	**el giro postal** postal ordery	**el telegrama** telegram	**el fax** fax

español • english

el buzón
postbox

el buzón
letterbox

el paquete
parcel

el mensajero
courier

el teléfono • telephone

el auricular
handset

**el contestador
automático**
answering machine

la base
base station

el teléfono inalámbrico
cordless phone

el videoteléfono
video phone

la cabina telefónica
telephone box

**el teléfono
inteligente**
smartphone

el teléfono móvil
mobile phone

el teclado
keypad

el auricular
receiver

las monedas devueltas
coin return

el teléfono público
payphone

---

vocabulario • vocabulary

la información telefónica directory enquiries	**el mensaje de texto (SMS)** text	**comunicando** engaged/busy	**¿Me podría dar el número de…?** Can you give me the number for…?
la llamada a cobro revertido reverse charge call	**el mensaje de voz** voice message	**apagado** disconnected	
marcar dial (v)	**el operador** operator	**la clave de acceso** passcode	**¿Cuál es el prefijo de larga distancia para llamar a…?** What is the dialling code for…?
contestar answer (v)	**la aplicación** app		**¡Mándame un mensaje de texto!** Text me!

el hotel • hotel
el vestíbulo • lobby

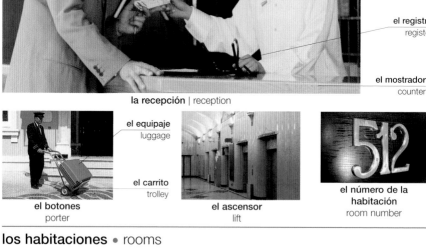

los mensajes
messages

el huésped
guest

la llave de la
habitación
room key

la casilla
pigeonhole

la recepcionista
receptionist

el registro
register

el mostrador
counter

la recepción | reception

el equipaje
luggage

el carrito
trolley

el botones
porter

el ascensor
lift

**el número de la
habitación**
room number

los habitaciones • rooms

**la habitación
individual**
single room

la habitación doble
double room

**la habitación con dos
camas individuales**
twin room

**el cuarto de baño
privado**
private bathroom

los servicios • services

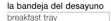
la bandeja del desayuno
breakfast tray

el servicio de limpieza
maid service

el servicio de lavandería
laundry service

el servicio de habitaciones | room service

el minibar
mini bar

el restaurante
restaurant

el gimnasio
gym

la piscina
swimming pool

---

vocabulario • vocabulary

la pensión completa full board	¿Tiene alguna habitación libre? Do you have any vacancies?	Quiero una habitación para tres días. I'd like a room for three nights.
la media pensión half board	Tengo una reserva. I have a reservation.	¿Cuánto cuesta la habitación por día? What is the charge per night?
la habitación con desayuno incluido bed and breakfast	Quiero una habitación individual. I'd like a single room.	¿Cuándo tengo que dejar la habitación? When do I have to vacate the room?

las compras
shopping

el centro comercial • shopping centre

el atrio
atrium

la segunda
planta
second floor

el letrero
sign

la primera
planta
first floor

el ascensor
lift

la escalera
mecánica
escalator

la planta
baja
ground floor

el cliente
customer

---

vocabulario • vocabulary

la sección de zapatería
shoe department

la sección infantil
children's department

**la sección de
equipajes**
luggage department

el directorio
store directory

el dependiente
sales assistant

**el servicio al
cliente**
customer services

los probadores
changing rooms

los aseos
toilets

**el cuarto para cambiar
a los bebés**
baby changing facilities

**¿Cuánto cuesta
esto?**
How much is this?

**¿Puedo cambiar
esto?**
May I exchange this?

---

los grandes almacenes • department store

la ropa de caballero
men's wear

la ropa de señora
women's wear

la lencería
lingerie

la perfumería
perfumery

los productos de belleza
beauty

la ropa de hogar
linen

el mobiliario para el hogar
home furnishings

la mercería
haberdashery

el menaje de hogar
kitchenware

las vajillas
china

los aparatos eléctricos
electrical goods

la iluminación
lighting

los artículos deportivos
sports

la juguetería
toys

la papelería
stationery

el supermercado
food hall

el supermercado • supermarket

el pasillo
aisle

el estante
shelf

la cinta transportadora
conveyer belt

el cajero
cashier

las ofertas
offers

la caja | checkout

el cliente
customer

la caja
till

la bolsa de la compra
shopping bag

la compra
groceries

el asa
handle

780863 185779

el código de barras
bar code

el carro
trolley

la cesta
basket

el escáner
scanner

la panadería
bakery

los lácteos
dairy

los cereales
cereals

las conservas
tinned food

la confitería
confectionery

la verdura
vegetables

la fruta
fruit

la carne y las aves
meat and poultry

el pescado
fish

la charcutería
deli

los congelados
frozen food

los platos preparados
convenience food

las bebidas
drinks

los productos de limpieza
household products

los artículos de aseo
toiletries

los artículos para el bebé
baby products

los electrodomésticos
electrical goods

la comida para animales
pet food

las revistas | magazines

la farmacia • chemist

la higiene femenina
feminine hygiene

el cuidado dental
dental care

los desodorantes
deodorants

las vitaminas
vitamins

el dispensario
dispensary

el farmacéutico
pharmacist

el jarabe para la tos
cough medicine

los remedios
de herbolario
herbal remedies

el cuidado de la piel
skin care

la loción para
después del sol
aftersun

la crema protectora
sunscreen

la crema
protectora total
sunblock

el repelente de insectos
insect repellent

la toallita húmeda
wet wipe

el pañuelo de papel
tissue

la compresa
sanitary towel

el tampón
tampon

el salvaslip
panty liner

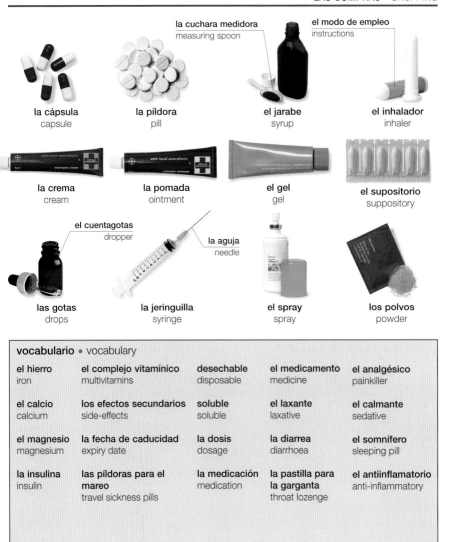

la cuchara medidora
measuring spoon

el modo de empleo
instructions

la cápsula
capsule

la píldora
pill

el jarabe
syrup

el inhalador
inhaler

la crema
cream

la pomada
ointment

el gel
gel

el supositorio
suppository

el cuentagotas
dropper

la aguja
needle

las gotas
drops

la jeringuilla
syringe

el spray
spray

los polvos
powder

vocabulario • vocabulary

el hierro iron	**el complejo vitamínico** multivitamins	**desechable** disposable	**el medicamento** medicine	**el analgésico** painkiller
el calcio calcium	**los efectos secundarios** side-effects	**soluble** soluble	**el laxante** laxative	**el calmante** sedative
el magnesio magnesium	**la fecha de caducidad** expiry date	**la dosis** dosage	**la diarrea** diarrhoea	**el somnífero** sleeping pill
la insulina insulin	**las píldoras para el mareo** travel sickness pills	**la medicación** medication	**la pastilla para la garganta** throat lozenge	**el antiinflamatorio** anti-inflammatory

la floristería • florist

las flores
flowers

el gladiolo
gladiolus

la azucena
lily

el iris
iris

la acacia
acacia

la margarita
daisy

el clavel
carnation

el crisantemo
chrysanthemum

la gypsofila
gypsophila

la maceta
pot plant

el alhelí
stocks

la gerbera
gerbera

el follaje
foliage

la rosa
rose

la fresia
freesia

el jarrón
vase

la orquídea
orchid

la peonía
peony

el ramo
bunch

el tallo
stem

el narciso
daffodil

el capullo
bud

el envoltorio
wrapping

el tulipán | tulip

los arreglos • arrangements

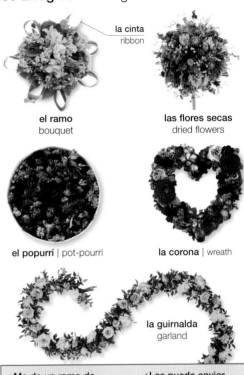

la cinta
ribbon

el ramo
bouquet

las flores secas
dried flowers

el popurrí | pot-pourri

la corona | wreath

la guirnalda
garland

¿Me da un ramo de…
por favor?
Can I have a bunch of…
please.

¿Me los puede envolver?
Can I have them
wrapped?

¿Puedo adjuntar un
mensaje?
Can I attach a message?

¿Los puede enviar
a…?
Can you send them
to….?

¿Cuánto tiempo
durarán éstos?
How long will these last?

¿Huelen?
Are they fragrant?

el vendedor de periódicos • newsagent

los cigarrillos
cigarettes

el paquete de tabaco
packet of cigarettes

los sellos
stamps

la tarjeta postal
postcard

el tebeo
comic

la revista
magazine

el periódico
newspaper

---

fumar • smoking

el tabaco
tobacco

el mechero
lighter

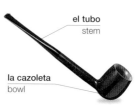

el tubo
stem

la cazoleta
bowl

la pipa
pipe

el puro
cigar

el vendedor de golosinas • confectioner

la caja de bombones
box of chocolates

la barrita
snack bar

las patata fritas
crisps

la tienda de golosinas | sweet shop

vocabulario • vocabulary	
el chocolate con leche milk chocolate	los caramelos duros boiled sweets
el chocolate negro plain chocolate	el caramelo caramel
el chocolate blanco white chocolate	la trufa truffle
las golosinas a granel pick and mix	la galleta biscuit

las golosinas • confectionery

el bombón
chocolate

la tableta de chocolate
chocolate bar

los caramelos
sweets

la piruleta
lollipop

el toffee
toffee

la nube
marshmallow

la pastilla de menta
mint

el turrón
nougat

el chicle
chewing gum

el caramelo blando
jellybean

la gominola
fruit gum

el regaliz
licquorice

las otras tiendas • other shops

la panadería
baker's

la confitería
cake shop

la carnicería
butcher's

la pescadería
fishmonger's

la verdulería
greengrocer's

el ultramarinos
grocer's

la zapatería
shoe shop

la ferretería
hardware shop

**la tienda de
antigüedades**
antiques shop

**la tienda de artículos
de regalo**
gift shop

la agencia de viajes
travel agent's

la joyería
jeweller's

la librería
book shop

la tienda de discos
record shop

la tienda de licores
off licence

la pajarería
pet shop

la tienda de muebles
furniture shop

la boutique
boutique

vocabulario • vocabulary

el vivero
garden centre

la lavandería
launderette

la tintorería
dry cleaner's

la herboristería
health food shop

la tienda de fotografía
camera shop

la tienda de artículos usados
second-hand shop

la agencia inmobiliaria
estate agent's

la tienda de materiales de arte
art shop

la sastrería
tailor's

la peluquería
hairdresser's

el mercado | market

los alimentos
food

la carne • meat

el cordero
lamb

el carnicero
butcher

el gancho
meat hook

el peso
scales

el afilador
knife sharpener

el bacon
bacon

las salchichas
sausages

el hígado
liver

vocabulario • vocabulary

el cerdo pork	**el venado** venison	**las asaduras** offal	**de granja** free range	**la carne roja** red meat
la vaca beef	**el conejo** rabbit	**curado** cured	**biológico** organic	**la carne magra** lean meat
la ternera veal	**la lengua** tongue	**ahumado** smoked	**la carne blanca** white meat	**el fiambre** cooked meat

los cortes • cuts

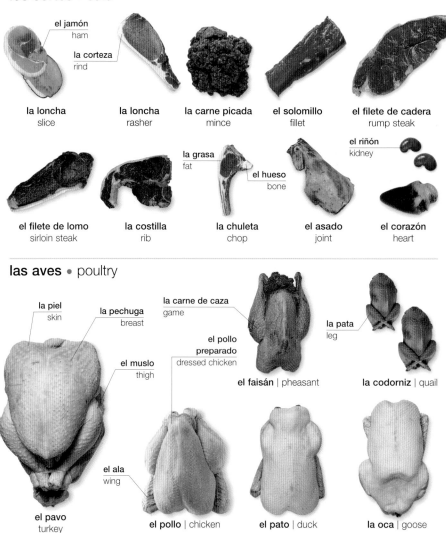

la loncha
slice

la loncha
rasher

la carne picada
mince

el solomillo
fillet

el filete de cadera
rump steak

el jamón
ham

la corteza
rind

la grasa
fat

el hueso
bone

el riñón
kidney

el filete de lomo
sirloin steak

la costilla
rib

la chuleta
chop

el asado
joint

el corazón
heart

las aves • poultry

la piel
skin

la pechuga
breast

el muslo
thigh

la carne de caza
game

el pollo
preparado
dressed chicken

la pata
leg

el ala
wing

el faisán | pheasant

la codorniz | quail

el pavo
turkey

el pollo | chicken

el pato | duck

la oca | goose

el pescado • fish

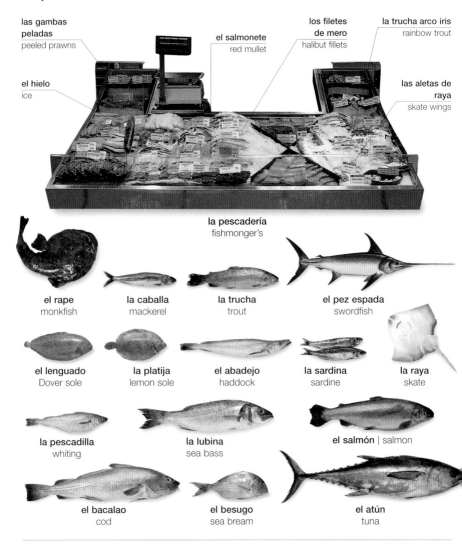

las gambas
peladas
peeled prawns

el hielo
ice

el salmonete
red mullet

los filetes
de mero
halibut fillets

la trucha arco iris
rainbow trout

las aletas de
raya
skate wings

la pescadería
fishmonger's

el rape
monkfish

la caballa
mackerel

la trucha
trout

el pez espada
swordfish

el lenguado
Dover sole

la platija
lemon sole

el abadejo
haddock

la sardina
sardine

la raya
skate

la pescadilla
whiting

la lubina
sea bass

el salmón | salmon

el bacalao
cod

el besugo
sea bream

el atún
tuna

el marisco • seafood

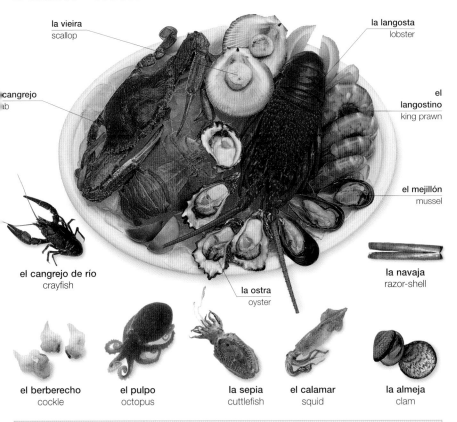

la vieira
scallop

la langosta
lobster

cangrejo
ab

el
langostino
king prawn

el mejillón
mussel

el cangrejo de río
crayfish

la ostra
oyster

la navaja
razor-shell

el berberecho
cockle

el pulpo
octopus

la sepia
cuttlefish

el calamar
squid

la almeja
clam

vocabulario • vocabulary

congelado	limpio	ahumado	sin escamas	en filetes	la rodaja	la cola	la espina	la escama
frozen	cleaned	smoked	descaled	filleted	steak	tail	bone	scale
fresco	salado	sin piel	sin espinas	el filete	el lomo	¿Me lo puede limpiar?		
fresh	salted	skinned	boned	fillet	loin	Will you clean it for me?		

las verduras 1 • vegetables 1

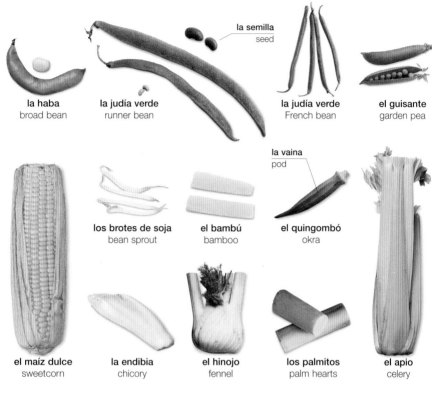

la semilla
seed

la haba
broad bean

la judía verde
runner bean

la judía verde
French bean

el guisante
garden pea

la vaina
pod

los brotes de soja
bean sprout

el bambú
bamboo

el quingombó
okra

el maíz dulce
sweetcorn

la endibia
chicory

el hinojo
fennel

los palmitos
palm hearts

el apio
celery

---

vocabulario • vocabulary

la hoja leaf	**la cabezuela** floret	**la punta** tip	**biológico** organic	**¿Vende verduras biológicas?** Do you sell organic vegetables?
el tallo stalk	**la almendra** kernel	**el centro** heart	**la bolsa de plástico** plastic bag	**¿Son productos locales?** Are these grown locally?

la rócula
rocket

el berro
watercress

el radicchio
radicchio

la col de bruselas
brussel sprout

la acelga
swiss chard

la col rizada
kale

la acedera
sorrel

la escarola
endive

el diente de león
dandelion

la espinaca
spinach

el colinabo
kohlrabi

la acelga china
pak-choi

la lechuga
lettuce

el brócoli
broccoli

la col
cabbage

la berza
spring greens

las verduras 2 • vegetables 2

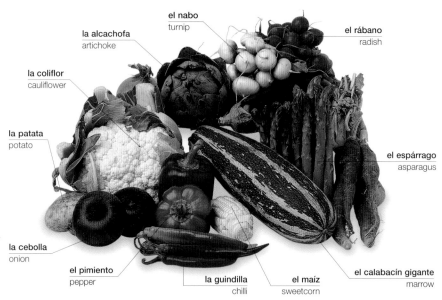

el nabo
turnip

la alcachofa
artichoke

el rábano
radish

la coliflor
cauliflower

la patata
potato

el espárrago
asparagus

la cebolla
onion

el pimiento
pepper

la guindilla
chilli

el maíz
sweetcorn

el calabacín gigante
marrow

vocabulario • vocabulary

el tomate cherry cherry tomato	**el apio-nabo** celeriac	**congelado** frozen	**amargo** bitter	**¿Me da un kilo de patatas, por favor?** Can I have one kilo of potatoes please?
la zanahoria carrot	**la raíz del taro** taro root	**crudo** raw	**firme** firm	**¿Cuánto vale el kilo?** What's the price per kilo?
el fruto del pan breadfruit	**la castaña de agua** water chestnut	**picante** hot (spicy)	**la pulpa** flesh	**¿Cómo se llaman ésos?** What are those called?
la patata nueva new potato	**la mandioca** cassava	**dulce** sweet	**la raíz** root	

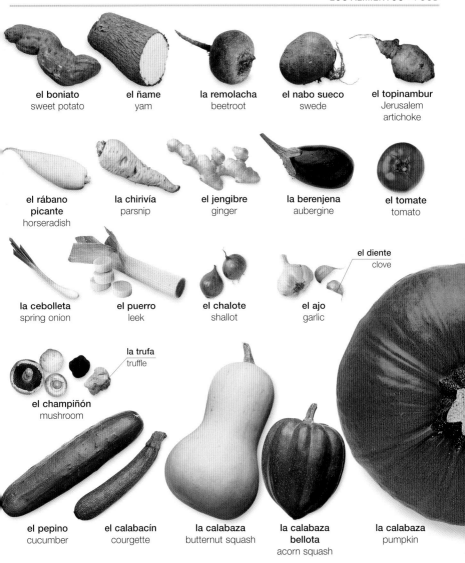

el boniato
sweet potato

el ñame
yam

la remolacha
beetroot

el nabo sueco
swede

el topinambur
Jerusalem artichoke

el rábano picante
horseradish

la chirivía
parsnip

el jengibre
ginger

la berenjena
aubergine

el tomate
tomato

la cebolleta
spring onion

el puerro
leek

el chalote
shallot

el ajo
garlic

el diente
clove

la trufa
truffle

el champiñón
mushroom

el pepino
cucumber

el calabacín
courgette

la calabaza
butternut squash

la calabaza bellota
acorn squash

la calabaza
pumpkin

la fruta 1 • fruit 1

los cítricos • citrus fruit

la naranja
orange

la mandarina clementina
clementine

la médula
pith

el ugli
ugli fruit

el pomelo
grapefruit

el gajo
segment

la mandarina satsuma
satsuma

la mandarina
tangerine

la corteza
zest

la lima
lime

el limón
lemon

el kumquat
kumquat

la fruta con hueso • stoned fruit

el melocotón
peach

la nectarina
nectarine

el albaricoque
apricot

la ciruela
plum

la cereza
cherry

la pera
pear

la manzana
apple

la cesta de fruta | basket of fruit

las bayas y los melones • berries and melons

la fresa
strawberry

la frambuesa
raspberry

el melón
melon

la uva
grapes

la mora
blackberry

la grosella
redcurrant

el arándano rojo
cranberry

la grosella negra
blackcurrant

la corteza
rind

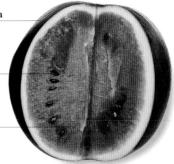

la pepita
seed

el arándano
blueberry

la grosella blanca
white currant

la pulpa
flesh

la sandía
watermelon

la frambuesa Logan
loganberry

la grosella espinosa
gooseberry

vocabulario • vocabulary

el ruibarbo rhubarb	**amargo** sour	**fresco** crisp	**sin pepitas** seedless	**¿Están maduros?** Are they ripe?
la fibra fibre	**fresco** fresh	**podrido** rotten	**el zumo** juice	**¿Puedo probar uno?** Can I try one?
dulce sweet	**jugoso** juicy	**la pulpa** pulp	**el corazón** core	**¿Hasta cuándo durarán?** How long will they keep?

la fruta 2 • fruit 2

el mango
mango

la piña
pineapple

el aguacate
avocado

la papaya
papaya

el melocotón
peach

el lichi
lychee

el kiwi
kiwifruit

el phisicallis
cape gooseberry

la pepita
pip

la piel
skin

el membrillo
quince

el maracuyá
passion fruit

el plátano
banana

la guayaba
guava

la granada
pomegranate

el caqui
persimmon

la feijoa
feijoa

el higo chumbo
prickly pear

la carambola
starfruit

el tomate de árbol
tamarillo

los frutos secos • nuts and dried fruit

el piñón
pine nut

el pistacho
pistachio

el anacardo
cashewnut

el cacahuete
peanut

la avellana
hazelnut

la nuez de Brasil
brazilnut

la pacana
pecan

la almendra
almond

la nuez
walnut

la castaña
chestnut

la macadamia
macadamia

el higo
fig

el dátil
date

la ciruela pasa
prune

la cáscara
shell

la pasa sultana
sultana

la pasa
raisin

la pasa de Corinto
currant

la pulpa
flesh

el coco
coconut

vocabulario • vocabulary

verde green	**duro** hard	**la almendra** kernel	**salado** salted	**tostado** roasted	**las frutas tropicales** tropical fruit	**pelado** shelled
maduro ripe	**blando** soft	**desecado** desiccated	**crudo** raw	**de temporada** seasonal	**la fruta escarchada** candied fruit	**entero** whole

los granos y las legumbres • grains and pulses

los granos • grains

el trigo
wheat

la avena
oats

la cebada
barley

el mijo
millet

el maíz
corn

la quinoa
quinoa

vocabulario • vocabulary

la semilla seed	**fresco** fresh	**integral** wholegrain
la cáscara husk	**perfumado** fragranced	**largo** long-grain
el grano kernel	**los cereales** cereal	**corto** short-grain
seco dry	**poner a remojo** soak (v)	**dede fácil cocción** easy cook

el arroz • rice

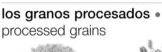

el arroz largo
white rice

el arroz integral
brown rice

el arroz salvaje
wild rice

el arroz bomba
pudding rice

los granos procesados • processed grains

el cuscús
couscous

el trigo partido
cracked wheat

la sémola
semolina

el salvado
bran

las alubias y los guisantes • beans and peas

la alubia blanca
butter beans

la alubia blanca pequeña
haricot beans

la alubia roja
red kidney beans

la alubia morada
aduki beans

las habas
broad beans

la semilla de soja
soya beans

la alubia de ojo negro
black-eyed beans

la alubia pinta
pinto beans

la alubia mung
mung beans

la alubia flageolet
flageolet beans

la lenteja castellana
brown lentils

la lenteja roja
red lentils

los guisantes tiernos
green peas

los garbanzos
chick peas

los guisantes secos
split peas

las semillas • seeds

la pipa de calabaza
pumpkin seed

la mostaza en grano
mustard seed

el carvi
caraway

la semilla de sésamo
sesame seed

la pipa de girasol
sunflower seed

las hierbas y las especias • herbs and spices

las especias • spices

la vainilla
vanilla

la nuez moscada
nutmeg

la macis
mace

la cúrcuma
turmeric

el comino
cumin

el ramillete aromático
bouquet garni

la pimienta de Jamaica
allspice

la pimienta en grano
peppercorn

el heno griego
fenugreek

la guindilla
chilli

entero
whole

machacado
crushed

el azafrán
saffron

el cardamono
cardamom

el curry en polvo
curry powder

molido
ground

el pimentón
paprika

laminado
flakes

el ajo
garlic

español • english

las hierbas • herbs

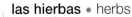

las ramas
sticks

la canela
cinnamon

la citronela
lemon grass

los clavos
cloves

el hinojo
fennel

**las semillas
de hinojo**
fennel seeds

el laurel
bay leaf

el perejil
parsley

los cebollinos
chives

la menta
mint

el tomillo
thyme

la salvia
sage

**el anís
estrellado**
star anise

el estragón
tarragon

la mejorana
marjoram

la albahaca
basil

el jengibre
ginger

el orégano
oregano

el cilantro
coriander

el eneldo
dill

el romero
rosemary

los alimentos embotellados •
bottled foods

el corcho
cork

el aceite de
girasol
sunflower oil

el aceite de nueces
walnut oil

el aceite de
semillas de uva
grapeseed oil

el aceite de
almendras
almond oil

el aceite de sésamo
sesame seed oil

el aceite de avellanas
hazelnut oil

el aceite de oliva
olive oil

las hierbas
herbs

el aceite
aromatizado
flavoured oil

los aceites
oils

las confituras • sweet spreads

el tarro
jar

el panal
honeycomb

la miel
compacta
set honey

la crema de
limón
lemon curd

la mermelada de
frambuesa
raspberry jam

la mermelada de
naranja
marmalade

la miel líquida
clear honey

el jarabe de
arce
maple syrup

los condimentos • condiments and spreads

la botella
bottle

el vinagre de sidra
cider vinegar

el vinagre
balsámico
balsamic vinegar

la mayonesa
mayonnaise

el ketchup
ketchup

**la mostaza
inglesa**
English mustard

**la mostaza
francesa**
French mustard

el chutney
chutney

el vinagre de malta
malt vinegar

el vinagre de vino
wine vinegar

el vinagre
vinegar

la salsa
sauce

**la mostaza en
grano**
wholegrain
mustard

---

el tarro hermético
sealed jar

**la mantequilla de
cacahuetes**
peanut butter

**el chocolate para
untar**
chocolate spread

**la fruta en
conserva**
preserved fruit

vocabulario • vocabulary

**el aceite
vegetal**
vegetable oil

**el aceite de
colza**
rapeseed oil

**el aceite de
maíz**
corn oil

**el aceite de
presión en frío**
cold-pressed oil

**el aceite de
cacahuete**
groundnut oil

los productos lácteos • dairy produce

el queso • cheese

la corteza
rind

el queso semicurado
semi-hard cheese

el queso rallado
grated cheese

el queso curado
hard cheese

el queso cremoso
semi-soft cheese

el requesón
cottage cheese

el queso cremoso
semicurado
cream cheese

el queso azul
blue cheese

el queso cremoso
soft cheese

el queso fresco | fresh cheese

la leche • milk

la leche
entera
whole milk

la leche semidesnatada
semi-skimmed milk

la leche desnatada
skimmed milk

el cartón de
leche
milk carton

la leche de vaca | cow's milk

la leche
de cabra
goat's milk

la leche
condensada
condensed milk

español • english

la mantequilla
butter

la margarina
margarine

la nata
cream

la nata líquida
single cream

la nata para montar
double cream

la nata montada
whipped cream

la nata agria
sour cream

el yogurt
yoghurt

el helado
ice-cream

los huevos • eggs

la yema
yolk

la clara
egg white

la cáscara
shell

la huevera
egg cup

el huevo pasado por agua
boiled egg

el huevo de gallina
hen's egg

el huevo de pato
duck egg

el huevo de oca
goose egg

el huevo de codorniz
quail egg

vocabulario • vocabulary

pasteurizado pasteurized	**sin grasa** fat free	**salado** salted	**la leche de oveja** sheep's milk	**la lactosa** lactose	**el batido** milkshake
sin pasteurizar unpasteurized	**la leche en polvo** powdered milk	**sin sal** unsalted	**el suero de la leche** buttermilk	**homogeneizado** homogenised	**el yogurt helado** frozen yoghurt

el pan y las harinas • breads and flours

el pan de molde
sliced bread

las semillas de amapola
poppy seeds

el pan de centeno
rye bread

la baguette
baguette

la panadería | bakery

haciendo pan • making bread

la harina blanca
white flour

la harina morena
brown flour

la harina integral
wholemeal flour

la levadura
yeast

cribar | sift (v)

mezclar | mix (v)

la masa
dough

amasar | knead (v)

hornear | bake (v)

la corteza
crust

la hogaza
loaf

la rebanada
slice

el pan blanco
white bread

el pan moreno
brown bread

el pan integral
wholemeal bread

el pan con grano
granary bread

el pan de maíz
corn bread

el pan al bicarbonato sódico
soda bread

el pan fermentado
sourdough bread

el pan sin levadura
flatbread

la rosquilla
bagel

el bollo
bap

el panecillo
roll

el plumcake
fruit bread

el pan con semillas
seeded bread

el naan
naan bread

el pan de pita
pitta bread

el biscote
crispbread

---

vocabulario • vocabulary

la harina con levadura self-raising flour	**la harina blanca** plain flour	**levar** prove (v)	**el pan rallado** breadcrumbs	**el rebanador** slicer
la harina para pan strong flour	**subir** rise (v)	**glasear** glaze (v)	**la barra** flute	**el panadero** baker

la repostería • cakes and desserts

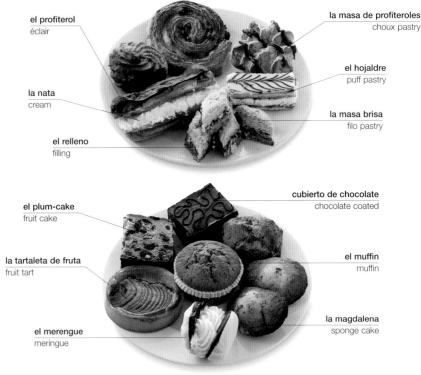

el profiterol
éclair

la masa de profiteroles
choux pastry

el hojaldre
puff pastry

la nata
cream

la masa brisa
filo pastry

el relleno
filling

cubierto de chocolate
chocolate coated

el plum-cake
fruit cake

la tartaleta de fruta
fruit tart

el muffin
muffin

el merengue
meringue

la magdalena
sponge cake

los pasteles | cakes

---

vocabulario • vocabulary

la crema pastelera	**el bollo**	**la masa**	**el arroz con leche**	**¿Puedo tomar un trozo?**
crème patisserie	bun	pastry	rice pudding	May I have a slice please?
el pastel de chocolate	**las natillas**	**el trozo**	**la celebración**	
chocolate cake	custard	slice	celebration	

los trocitos de chocolate
chocolate chip

las soletillas
sponge fingers

la florentina
florentine

el postre de soletillas, gelatina de frutas y nata
trifle

las galletas | biscuits

la mousse
mousse

el sorbete
sorbet

el pastel de nata
cream pie

el flan
crème caramel

las tartas para celebraciones • celebration cakes

el último piso
top tier

la cinta
ribbon

la decoración
decoration

las velas de cumpleaños
birthday candles

apagar
blow out (v)

el primer piso
bottom tier

la alcorza
icing

el mazapán
marzipan

la tarta nupcial | wedding cake

la tarta de cumpleaños | birthday cake

la charcutería • delicatessen

el fiambre
spicy sausage

la quiche
flan

el vinagre
vinegar

el aceite
oil

la carne fresca
uncooked meat

el mostrador
counter

el salami
salami

el salchichón
pepperoni

el paté
pâté

la mozzarella
mozzarella

el brie
brie

el queso de cabra
goat's cheese

el cheddar
cheddar

el parmesano
parmesan

el camembert
camembert

la corteza
rind

el queso de bola
edam

el manchego
manchego

los pasteles de carne
pies

la aceituna negra
black olive

la guindilla
chili

la salsa
sauce

el panecillo
bread roll

el fiambre
cooked meat

la aceituna verde
green olive

el jamón
ham

el mostrador de bocadillos
sandwich counter

el pescado ahumado
smoked fish

las alcaparras
capers

la corteza
chorizo

el jamón serrano
prosciutto

la aceituna rellena
stuffed olive

vocabulario • vocabulary

en aceite in oil	adobado marinated	ahumado smoked
en salmuera in brine	salado salted	curado cured

Coja un número, por favor.
Take a number please.

¿Puedo probar un poco de eso?
Can I try some of that please?

¿Me pone seis lonchas de aquél?
May I have six slices of that please?

las bebidas • drinks

el agua • water

el agua embotellada
bottled water

con gas
sparkling

sin gas
still

el agua mineral
mineral water

el agua del grifo
tap water

la tónica
tonic water

la soda
soda water

las bebidas calientes •
hot drinks

la bolsita de té
teabag

el té en hoja
loose leaf tea

el té
tea

los granos
beans

el café molido
ground coffee

el café
coffee

el chocolate
caliente
hot chocolate

la bebida
malteada
malted drink

los refrescos • soft drinks

la pajita
straw

el zumo de
tomate
tomato juice

el zumo de uva
grape juice

la limonada
lemonade

la naranjada
orangeade

la cola
cola

las bebidas alcohólicas • alcoholic drinks

la ginebra
gin

la lata
can

la cerveza
beer

la sidra
cider

la cerveza amarga
bitter

la cerveza negra
stout

el vodka
vodka

el whisky
whisky

el ron
rum

el coñac
brandy

el oporto
port

seco
dry

el vino de jerez
sherry

el campari
campari

rosado
rosé

blanco
white

tinto
red

el vino
wine

el licor
liqueur

el tequila
tequila

el champán
champagne

comer fuera
eating out

la cafetería · café

la carta
menu

el toldo
awning

la sombrilla
umbrella

la cafetería con mesas fuera | pavement café

la terraza
terrace café

la máquina del café
coffee machine

el camarero
waiter

la mesa
table

el bar | snack bar

el café · coffee

el café con leche
white coffee

el café solo
black coffee

el cacao en polvo
cocoa powder

la espuma
froth

el café de cafetera eléctrica
filter coffee

el café solo
espresso

el cappuccino
cappuccino

el café con hielo
iced coffee

el té • tea

la infusión
herbal tea

la manzanilla
camomile tea

el té verde
green tea

el té con leche
tea with milk

el té sólo
black tea

el té con limón
tea with lemon

la menta poleo
mint tea

el té con hielo
iced tea

los zumos y los batidos • juices and milkshakes

el batido de chocolate
chocolate milkshake

el batido
de fresa
strawberry
milkshake

el batido
de café
coffee
milkshake

el zumo de
naranja
orange juice

el zumo de
manzana
apple juice

el zumo de
piña
pineapple juice

el zumo de
tomate
tomato juice

la comida • food

la bola
scoop

el pan integral
brown bread

el sandwich tostado
toasted sandwich

la ensalada
salad

el helado
ice cream

el pastel
pastry

el bar • bar

el medidor óptico
optic

los vasos
glasses

la caja
till

el camarero
bartender

el grifo de cerveza
beer tap

la máquina
del café
coffee machine

la champanera
ice bucket

el taburete
bar stool

el cenicero
ashtray

el posavasos
coaster

la barra
bar counter

el abrebotellas
bottle opener

la palanca
lever

el sacacorchos | corkscrew

las pinzas
tongs

el agitador
stirrer

el medidor
measure

la coctelera | cocktail shaker

la jarra
pitcher

el cubito de hielo
ice cube

el gin tonic
gin and tonic

**el whiskey escocés
con agua**
scotch and water

el ron con cola
rum and coke

el vodka con naranja
vodka and orange

el martini
martini

el cóctel
cocktail

el vino
wine

la cerveza | beer

doble
double

con hielo y limón
ice and lemon

sencillo
single

un trago
a shot

la medida
measure

sin hielo
without ice

con hielo
with ice

los aperitivos • bar snacks

los anacardos
cashew nuts

los cacahuetes
peanuts

las almendras
almonds

las patatas fritas | crisps

los frutos secos | nuts

las aceitunas | olives

el restaurante • restaurant

el cubierto
table setting

el ayudante
del chef
commis chef

la copa
glass

el chef
chef

la bandeja
tray

la cocina
kitchen

el camarero
waiter

---

vocabulario • vocabulary

la lista de vinos wine list	**a la carta** à la carte	**el precio** price	**la propina** tip	**el buffet** buffet	**la pimienta** pepper
el menú de la cena evening menu	**los platos del día** specials	**la cuenta** bill	**servicio incluido** service included	**la sal** salt	**el cliente** customer
			servicio no incluido service not included	**el bar** bar	
el menú de la comida lunch menu	**el carrito de los postres** sweet trolley	**el recibo** receipt			

la carta
menu

el menú para niños
child's meal

pedir
order (v)

pagar
pay (v)

los platos • courses

el aperitivo
apéritif

el entrante
starter

la sopa
soup

el plato principal
main course

el acompañamiento
side order

el postre | dessert

el café | coffee

Una mesa para dos, por favor.
A table for two please.

¿Podría ver la carta/lista de vinos, por favor?
Can I see the menu/winelist please?

¿Hay menú del día?
Is there a fixed price menu?

¿Tiene platos vegetarianos?
Do you have any vegetarian dishes?

¿Me podría traer la cuenta/un recibo?
Could I have the bill/a receipt please?

¿Podemos pagar por separado?
Can we pay separately?

¿Dónde están los servicios, por favor?
Where are the toilets, please?

---

la comida rápida • fast food

la hamburguesa
burger

la pajita
straw

el refresco
soft drink

las patatas fritas
french fries

la servilleta de
papel
paper napkin

la bandeja
tray

la hamburguesa con patatas fritas
burger meal

la pizza
pizza

la lista de precios
price list

la lata de bebida
canned drink

la entrega a domicilio
home delivery

el puesto callejero
street stall

vocabulario •
vocabulary

la pizzería
pizza parlour

la hamburguesería
burger bar

el menú
menu

para comer en el local
eat-in

para llevar
take-away

recalentar
re-heat (v)

el ketchup
tomato sauce

· · · · · · · · · · · · · · · · · · · ·

¿Me lo pone para llevar?
Can I have that to go
please?

¿Entregan a domicilio?
Do you deliver?

el bollo
bun

la mostaza
mustard

la salchicha
sausage

la hamburguesa
hamburger

**la hamburguesa de
pollo**
chicken burger

**la hamburguesa
vegetariana**
veggie burger

el perrito caliente
hot dog

el relleno
filling

el bocadillo
sandwich

el club sandwich
club sandwich

el sandwich abierto
open sandwich

el taco
wrap

la salsa
sauce

salado
savoury

dulce
sweet

los ingredientes
topping

el pincho moruno
kebab

las porciones de pollo
chicken nuggets

la crêpe | crêpes

el pescado y las patatas fritas
fish and chips

las costillas
ribs

el pollo frito
fried chicken

la pizza
pizza

el desayuno • breakfast

la leche
milk

los
cereales
cereal

la mermelada
jam

la fruta
desecada
dried fruit

el jamón
ham

el queso
cheese

la galleta de
centeno
crispbread

el buffet de desayuno
breakfast buffet

el paté
pâté

la mantequilla
butter

la mermelada de naranja
marmalade

el zumo de frutas
fruit juice

el café
coffee

el cacao
hot chocolate

el croissant
croissant

el té
tea

la mesa del desayuno | breakfast table

las bebidas | drinks

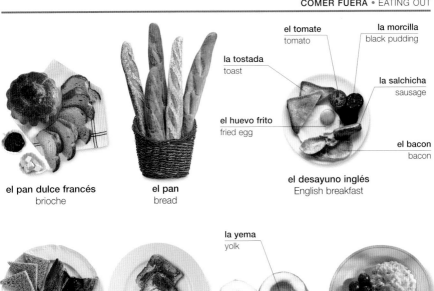

el tomate
tomato

la morcilla
black pudding

la tostada
toast

la salchicha
sausage

el huevo frito
fried egg

el bacon
bacon

el pan dulce francés
brioche

el pan
bread

el desayuno inglés
English breakfast

los arenques ahumados
kippers

la torrija
french toast

la yema
yolk

el huevo pasado por agua
boiled egg

los huevos revueltos
scrambled eggs

la nata
cream

los crepes
pancakes

los gofres
waffles

el yogurt de frutas
fruit yoghurt

las gachas de avena
porridge

la fruta fresca
fresh fruit

la comida principal • dinner

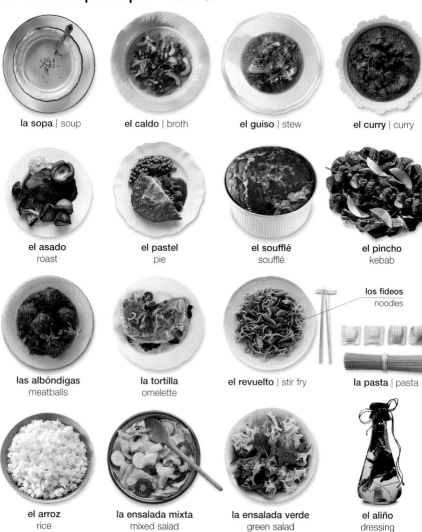

la sopa | soup

el caldo | broth

el guiso | stew

el curry | curry

el asado
roast

el pastel
pie

el soufflé
soufflé

el pincho
kebab

las albóndigas
meatballs

la tortilla
omelette

el revuelto | stir fry

los fideos
noodles

la pasta | pasta

el arroz
rice

la ensalada mixta
mixed salad

la ensalada verde
green salad

el aliño
dressing

las técnicas • techniques

relleno | stuffed

en salsa | in sauce

a la plancha | grilled

adobado | marinated

escalfado | poached

hecho puré | mashed

cocido en el horno
baked

frito con poco aceite
pan fried

frito
fried

en vinagre
pickled

ahumado
smoked

frito con mucho aceite
deep fried

en almíbar
in syrup

aliñado
dressed

al vapor
steamed

curado
cured

el estudio
study

el colegio • school

la pizarra
whiteboard

la profesora
teacher

la cartera
school bag

la alumna
pupil

el pupitre
desk

la tiza
chalk

el aula | classroom

la colegiala
schoolgirl

el colegial
schoolboy

---

vocabulario • vocabulary

la historia history	**el arte** art	**la física** physics
la geografía geography	**la música** music	**la química** chemistry
la literatura literature	**las ciencias** science	**la biología** biology
los idiomas languages	**las matemáticas** maths	**la educación física** physical education

las actividades • activities

leer | read (v)

escribir | write (v)

deletrear
spell (v)

dibujar
draw (v)

la punta
nib

el lápiz de colores
colouring pencil

el sacapuntas
pencil
sharpener

el proyector digital
digital projector

el bolígrafo
pen

el lápiz
pencil

la goma
rubber

el cuaderno
notebook

el libro de texto | textbook

el estuche
pencil case

la regla
ruler

preguntar
question (v)

contestar
answer (v)

discutir
discuss (v)

aprender
learn (v)

vocabulario • vocabulary

el director head teacher	**la respuesta** answer	**la nota** grade
la lección lesson	**los deberes** homework	**el curso** year
la pregunta question	**la redacción** essay	**el diccionario** dictionary
tomar apuntes take notes (v)	**el examen** examination	**la enciclopedia** encyclopedia

las matemáticas • maths

las formas • shapes

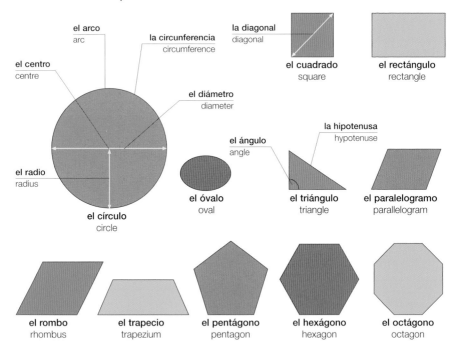

el arco
arc

la circunferencia
circumference

la diagonal
diagonal

el cuadrado
square

el rectángulo
rectangle

el centro
centre

el diámetro
diameter

la hipotenusa
hypotenuse

el ángulo
angle

el radio
radius

el óvalo
oval

el triángulo
triangle

el paralelogramo
parallelogram

el círculo
circle

el rombo
rhombus

el trapecio
trapezium

el pentágono
pentagon

el hexágono
hexagon

el octágono
octagon

los cuerpos geométricos • solids

el lado
side

el ápice
apex

la base
base

el cono
cone

el cilindro
cylinder

el cubo
cube

la pirámide
pyramid

la esfera
sphere

las líneas • lines

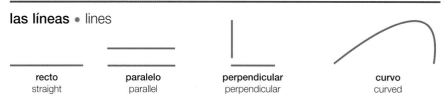

| **recto** | **paralelo** | **perpendicular** | **curvo** |
| straight | parallel | perpendicular | curved |

las medidas • measurements

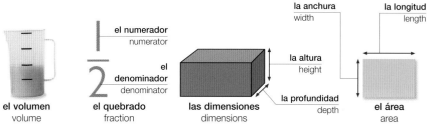

el volumen
volume

el quebrado
fraction

el numerador
numerator

el denominador
denominator

las dimensiones
dimensions

la anchura
width

la longitud
length

la altura
height

la profundidad
depth

el área
area

los materiales • equipment

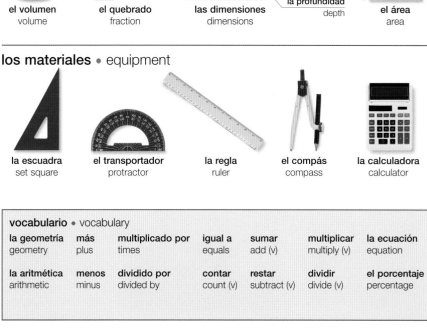

la escuadra
set square

el transportador
protractor

la regla
ruler

el compás
compass

la calculadora
calculator

---

vocabulario • vocabulary

la geometría	**más**	**multiplicado por**	**igual a**	**sumar**	**multiplicar**	**la ecuación**
geometry	plus	times	equals	add (v)	multiply (v)	equation
la aritmética	**menos**	**dividido por**	**contar**	**restar**	**dividir**	**el porcentaje**
arithmetic	minus	divided by	count (v)	subtract (v)	divide (v)	percentage

---

las ciencias • science

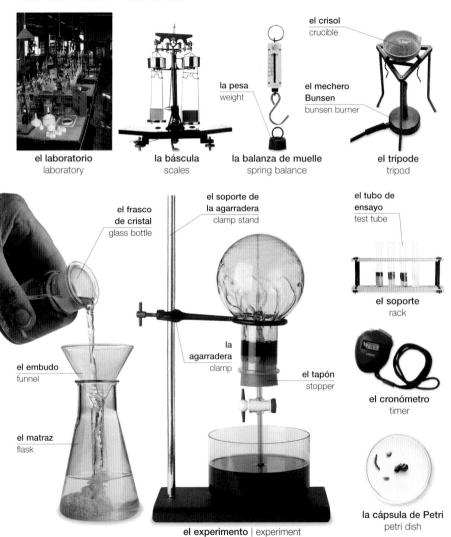

el laboratorio
laboratory

la báscula
scales

la pesa
weight

la balanza de muelle
spring balance

el crisol
crucible

el mechero Bunsen
bunsen burner

el trípode
tripod

el frasco de cristal
glass bottle

el soporte de la agarradera
clamp stand

el tubo de ensayo
test tube

el soporte
rack

el embudo
funnel

la agarradera
clamp

el tapón
stopper

el cronómetro
timer

el matraz
flask

la cápsula de Petri
petri dish

el experimento | experiment

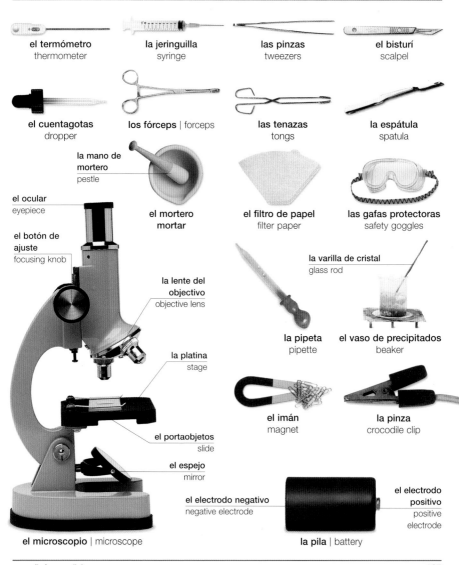

el termómetro
thermometer

la jeringuilla
syringe

las pinzas
tweezers

el bisturí
scalpel

el cuentagotas
dropper

los fórceps | forceps

las tenazas
tongs

la espátula
spatula

la mano de mortero
pestle

el mortero
mortar

el filtro de papel
filter paper

las gafas protectoras
safety goggles

el ocular
eyepiece

el botón de ajuste
focusing knob

la lente del objectivo
objective lens

la platina
stage

el portaobjetos
slide

el espejo
mirror

la varilla de cristal
glass rod

la pipeta
pipette

el vaso de precipitados
beaker

el imán
magnet

la pinza
crocodile clip

el microscopio | microscope

el electrodo negativo
negative electrode

el electrodo positivo
positive electrode

la pila | battery

la enseñanza superior • college

la secretaría
admissions

el campo de deportes
sports field

el refectorio
refectory

el colegio mayor
hall of residence

el centro de salud
health centre

el campus | campus

vocabulario • vocabulary

la sala de lecturas reading room	**el libro** book	**el préstamo** loan
la lista de lecturas reading list	**reservar** reserve (v)	**el título** title
la tarjeta de la biblioteca library card	**coger prestado** borrow (v)	**la información** enquiries
la fecha de devolución return date	**renovar** renew (v)	**el pasillo** aisle

la bibliotecaria
librarian

el mostrador de préstamos
loans desk

la estantería
bookshelf

el periódico
periodical

la revista
journal

la biblioteca | library

el estudiante
undergraduate

el profesor
lecturer

la licenciada
graduate

la toga
robe

el anfiteatro
lecture theatre

la ceremonia de graduación
graduation ceremony

las escuelas • schools

la modelo
model

la escuela de Bellas Artes
art college

el conservatorio
music school

la academia de danza
dance academy

vocabulario • vocabulary

la beca scholarship	**la investigación** research	**la tesina** dissertation	**la medicina** medicine	**la política** politics
el diploma diploma	**el máster** masters	**el departamento** department	**la zoología** zoology	**la literatura** literature
la carrera degree	**el doctorado** doctorate	**el derecho** law	**la física** physics	**la historia del arte** history of art
posgrado postgraduate	**la tesis** thesis	**la ingeniería** engineering	**la filosofía** philosophy	**las ciencias económicas** economics

el trabajo
work

la oficina 1 • office 1

la bandeja de entrada
in-tray

la pantalla
monitor

el portabolígrafos
desktop organizer

el cuaderno
notebook

el ordenador portátil
laptop

la bandeja de salida
out-tray

el cajón
drawer

el escritorio
desk

la silla giratoria
swivel chair

la papelera
wastebasket

el archivador
filing cabinet

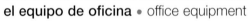

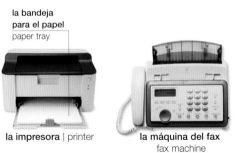

---

el equipo de oficina • office equipment

la bandeja para el papel
paper tray

la impresora | printer

la máquina del fax
fax machine

vocabulario • vocabulary	
imprimir print (v)	**ampliar** enlarge (v)
fotocopiar copy (v)	**reducir** reduce (v)

Necesito hacer unas fotocopias.
I need to make some copies.

los materiales de oficina • office supplies

la nota con saludos
compliments slip

el membrete
letterhead

el sobre
envelope

la caja archivador
box file

el divisor
divider

el rótulo
tab

la tablilla con sujetapapeles
clipboard

el bloc de apuntes
note pad

el archivador suspendido
hanging file

la carpeta de acordeón
concertina file

la carpeta de anillas
lever arch file

el papel celo
sticky tape

la almohadilla de la tinta
ink pad

las grapas
staples

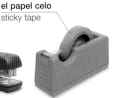

la agenda
personal organizer

la grapadora
stapler

el soporte del papel celo
tape dispenser

la perforadora
hole punch

el sello
rubber stamp

la chincheta
drawing pin

la goma elástica
rubber band

el clip
bulldog clip

el sujetapapeles
paper clip

el tablón de anuncios | notice board

la oficina 2 • office 2

la pizarra
flipchart

el caballete
easel

la propuesta
proposal

el director
manager

el acta
minutes

el informe
report

el ejecutivo
executive

la reunión | meeting

vocabulario • vocabulary

la sala de reuniones
meeting room

asistir
attend (v)

el orden del día
agenda

presidir
chair (v)

¿A qué hora es la reunión?
What time is the meeting?

¿Cuál es su horario de oficina?
What are your office hours?

la oradora
speaker

la presentación | presentation

los negocios • business

el hombre de negocios
businessman

la mujer de negocios
businesswoman

la comida de negocios
business lunch

el viaje de negocios
business trip

la cita
appointment

la agenda | diary

el director general
managing director

la clienta
client

el trato
business deal

vocabulario • vocabulary

la empresa company	el departamento de ventas sales department	el departamento legal legal department
la sucursal branch	el departamento de contabilidad accounts department	el departamento de atención al cliente customer service department
el personal staff	el departamento de márketing marketing department	el departamento de recursos humanos personnel department
la nómina payroll	la oficina central head office	el sueldo salary

el ordenador • computer

la impresora
printer

la pantalla
screen

el escáner
scanner

el ordenador portátil
laptop

el altavoz
speaker

la tecla
key

el teclado
keyboard

el ratón
mouse

el hardware
hardware

la llave de memoria
memory stick

el disco duro externo
external hard drive

vocabulario • vocabulary

la memoria memory	**el software** software	**el servidor** server
el RAM RAM	**la aplicación** application	**el puerto** port
los bytes bytes	**el programa** program	**el procesador** processor
el sistema system	**la red** network	**el cable de alimentación** power cable

el iPad
iPad

el teléfono inteligente
smartphone

el escritorio • desktop

la fuente
font

la barra del menú
menubar

el fichero
file

el icono
icon

la barra
de acceso
toolbar

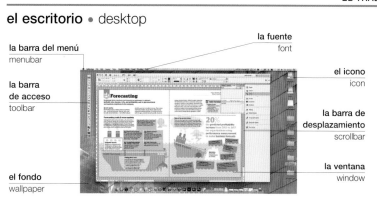

la barra de
desplazamiento
scrollbar

la carpeta
folder

la ventana
window

el fondo
wallpaper

la papelera
trash

el internet • internet

el navegador
browser

navegar
browse (v)

el correo electrónico • email

la dirección
electrónica
email address

la bandeja
de entrada
inbox

el sitio web
website

---

vocabulario • vocabulary

conectar connect (v)	**la cuenta de correo** email account	**en línea** on-line	**bajar** download (v)	**enviar** send (v)	**guardar** save (v)
instalar install (v)	**el proveedor de servicios** service provider	**entrar en el sistema** log on (v)	**el documento adjunto** attachment	**recibir** receive (v)	**buscar** search (v)

---

los medios de comunicación • media

el estudio de televisión • television studio

el plató
set

el presentador
presenter

el foco
light

la cámara
camera

la grúa de la cámara
camera crane

el cámara
cameraman

vocabulario • vocabulary

el canal channel	**el documental** documentary	**la prensa** press	**la telenovela** soap	**emitir** broadcast (v)	**en directo** live
la programación programming	**las noticias** news	**la serie televisiva** television series	**el concurso** game show	**los dibujos animados** cartoon	**en diferido** prerecorded

el entrevistador
interviewer

la reportera
reporter

el autocue
autocue

**la presentadora de
las noticias**
newsreader

los actores
actors

la jirafa
sound boom

la claqueta
clapper board

el plató de rodaje
film set

la radio • radio

el técnico de **la mesa de** **el micrófono**
sonido **mezclas** microphone
sound technician mixing desk

el estudio de grabación | recording studio

vocabulario • vocabulary

la estación de radio **la frecuencia**
radio station frequency

el pinchadiscos **la onda corta**
DJ short wave

la emisión **la onda media**
broadcast medium wave

la longitud de onda **el volumen**
wavelength volume

la onda larga **sintonizar**
long wave tune (v)

analógico **digital**
analog digital

el derecho • law

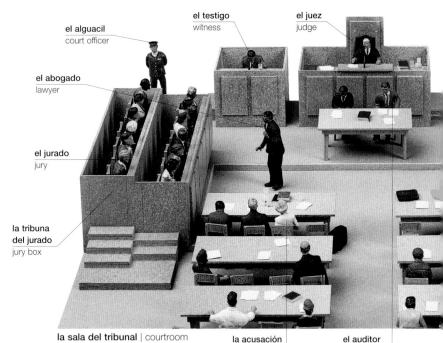

el testigo
witness

el juez
judge

el alguacil
court officer

el abogado
lawyer

el jurado
jury

la tribuna del jurado
jury box

la sala del tribunal | courtroom

la acusación
prosecution

el auditor
court official

---

vocabulario • vocabulary

el bufete lawyer's office	**la citación** summons	**la orden judicial** writ	**el juicio** court case
la asesoría jurídica legal advice	**la declaración** statement	**la fecha del juicio** court date	**el cargo** charge
el cliente client	**la orden judicial** warrant	**cómo se declara el acusado** plea	**el acusado** accused

la taquígrafa
stenographer

el sospechoso
suspect

el acusado
defendant

la defensa
defence

el criminal
criminal

el retrato robot
photofit

los antecedentes
criminal record

el funcionario de prisiones
prison guard

la celda
cell

la cárcel
prison

vocabulario • vocabulary

la prueba evidence	**culpable** guilty	**la fianza** bail	**Quiero ver a un abogado.** I want to see a lawyer.
el veredicto verdict	**absuelto** acquitted	**la apelación** appeal	**¿Dónde está el juzgado?** Where is the courthouse?
inocente innocent	**la sentencia** sentence	**la libertad condicional** parole	**¿Puedo pagar la fianza?** Can I post bail?

la granja 1 • farm 1

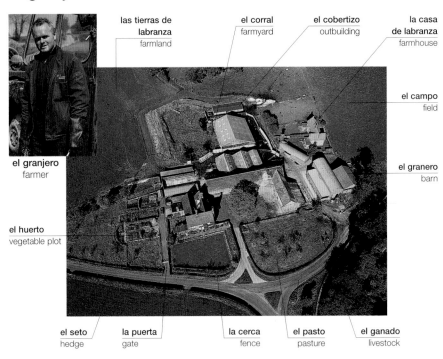

las tierras de labranza
farmland

el corral
farmyard

el cobertizo
outbuilding

la casa de labranza
farmhouse

el campo
field

el granjero
farmer

el granero
barn

el huerto
vegetable plot

el seto
hedge

la puerta
gate

la cerca
fence

el pasto
pasture

el ganado
livestock

el cultivador
cultivator

el tractor | tractor

la cosechadora | combine harvester

los tipos de granja • types of farm

la cosecha
crop

la granja de tierras cultivables
arable farm

la vaquería
dairy farm

el rebaño
flock

la granja de ganado ovino
sheep farm

la granja avícola
poultry farm

la vid
vine

la granja de ganado porcino
pig farm

la piscifactoría
fish farm

la granja de frutales
fruit farm

el viñedo
vineyard

las actividades • actions

el surco
furrow

arar
plough (v)

sembrar
sow (v)

ordeñar
milk (v)

dar de comer
feed (v)

regar | water (v)

recolectar | harvest (v)

vocabulario • vocabulary

el herbicida	**la manada**	**el comedero**
herbicide	herd	trough
el pesticida	**el silo**	**plantar**
pesticide	silo	plant (v)

la granja 2 • farm 2

las cosechas • crops

el trigo
wheat

el maíz
corn

la cebada
barley

la colza
rapeseed

el girasol
sunflower

la bala
bale

el heno
hay

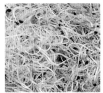
la alfalfa
alfalfa

el tabaco
tobacco

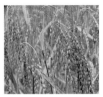
el arroz
rice

el té
tea

el café
coffee

el espantapájaros
scarecrow

el lino
flax

la caña de azúcar
sugarcane

el algodón
cotton

el ganado • livestock

el cerdito
piglet

el ternero
calf

el cerdo
pig

la vaca
cow

el toro
bull

la oveja
sheep

el cordero
lamb

el cabrito
kid

la cabra
goat

el potro
foal

el caballo
horse

el burro
donkey

el polluelo
chick

la gallina
chicken

el gallo
cockerel

el pavo
turkey

el patito
duckling

el pato
duck

el establo
stable

el redil
pen

el gallinero
chicken coop

la pocilga
pigsty

la construcción • construction

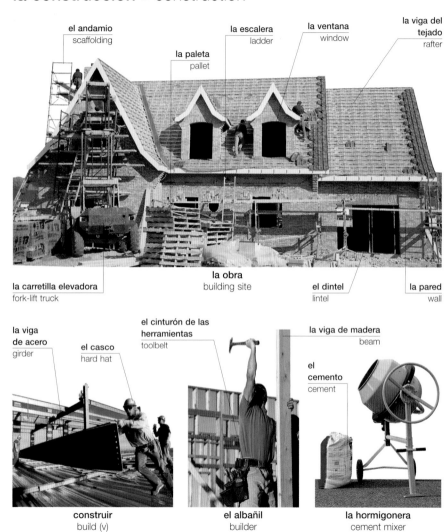

el andamio
scaffolding

la paleta
pallet

la escalera
ladder

la ventana
window

la viga del
tejado
rafter

la carretilla elevadora
fork-lift truck

la obra
building site

el dintel
lintel

la pared
wall

la viga
de acero
girder

el casco
hard hat

el cinturón de las
herramientas
toolbelt

la viga de madera
beam

el
cemento
cement

construir
build (v)

el albañil
builder

la hormigonera
cement mixer

los materiales • materials

el ladrillo
brick

la madera
timber

la teja
roof tile

el bloque de hormigón
concrete block

las herramientas • tools

la argamasa
mortar

la paleta
trowel

el nivel
spirit level

el mango
handle

el mazo
sledgehammer

el pico
pickaxe

la pala
shovel

la maquinaria • machinery

la apisonadora
roller

el camión volquete
dumper truck

el soporte
support

el
gancho
hook

la grúa | crane

las obras • roadworks

el asfalto
tarmac

el cono
cone

**el martillo
neumático**
pneumatic drill

el
revestimiento
resurfacing

**la excavadora
mecánica**
mechanical digger

las profesiones 1 • occupations 1

el carpintero
carpenter

el electricista
electrician

el fontanero
plumber

el albañil
builder

el jardinero
gardener

la
aspiradora
vacuum
cleaner

el empleado de la limpieza
cleaner

el mecánico
mechanic

el carnicero
butcher

la pescadera
fishmonger

el frutero
greengrocer

la florista
florist

el peluquero
hairdresser

el barbero
barber

el joyero
jeweller

la dependienta
shop assistant

la agente inmobiliario
estate agent

el óptico
optician

la mascarilla
mask
la dentista
dentist

el médico
doctor

la farmacéutica
pharmacist

la enfermera
nurse

la veterinaria
vet

el agricultor
farmer

el pescador
fisherman

la metralleta
machine-gun

la placa de
identificación
identity badge

el uniforme
uniform

**el guardia de
seguridad**
security guard

el marino
sailor

el soldado
soldier

el policía
policeman

el bombero
fireman

las profesiones 2 • occupations 2

la maqueta
model

el abogado
lawyer

el contable
accountant

el arquitecto
architect

la científica
scientist

la profesora
teacher

el bibliotecario
librarian

la recepcionista
receptionist

la
cartera
mailbag

el cartero
postman

el conductor de autobús
bus driver

el camionero
lorry driver

el taxista
taxi driver

el piloto
pilot

la azafata
air stewardess

la agente de viajes
travel agent

el gorro de cocinero
chef's hat

el chef
chef

el tutú
tutu

el músico
musician

la bailarina
dancer

la actriz
actress

la cantante
singer

la camarera
waitress

el camarero
barman

el deportista
sportsman

el escultor
sculptor

las notas
notes

la pintora
painter

el fotógrafo
photographer

la presentadora
newsreader

el periodista
journalist

la redactora
editor

el diseñador
designer

la modista
seamstress

el sastre
tailor

el transporte
transport
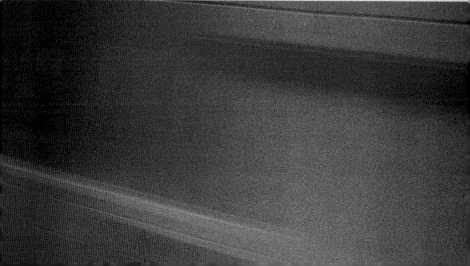

las carreteras • roads

la autopista
motorway

la caseta de
peaje
toll booth

las señales
horizontales
road markings

la vía de acceso
slip road

de sentido único
one-way

la línea divisoria
divider

la salida
junction

el semáforo
traffic light

el carril para el
tráfico lento
inside lane

el carril central
middle lane

el carril de
adelantamiento
outside lane

la vía de salida
exit ramp

el tráfico
traffic

el paso elevado
flyover

el arcén
hard shoulder

el camión
lorry

la mediana
central reservation

el paso subterráneo
underpass

el paso de peatones
pedestrian crossing

el teléfono de emergencia
emergency phone

el aparcamiento para minusválidos
disabled parking

el atasco de tráfico
traffic jam

el navegador por satélite
satnav

el parquímetro
parking meter

el policía de tráfico
traffic policeman

vocabulario • vocabulary

la glorieta roundabout	**dar marcha atrás** reverse (v)	**remolcar** tow away (v)
el desvío diversion	**conducir** drive (v)	**la autovía** dual carriageway
aparcar park (v)	**las obras** roadworks	**¿Es ésta la carretera hacia...?** Is this the road to...?
adelantar overtake (v)	**la barrera de seguridad** crash barrier	**¿Dónde se puede aparcar?** Where can I park?

las señales de tráfico • road signs

prohibido el paso
no entry

el límite de velocidad
speed limit

peligro
hazard

prohibido parar
no stopping

no torcer a la derecha
no right turn

el autobús • bus

el asiento del conductor
driver's seat

la barandilla
handrail

la puerta automática
automatic door

la rueda delantera
front wheel

el portaequipajes
luggage hold

la puerta | door

el autocar | coach

los tipos de autobuses • types of buses

el número de ruta
route number

el conductor
driver

el autobús de dos pisos
double-decker bus

el tranvía
tram

el trolebús
trolley bus

el autobús escolar | school bus

la ventana
window

el botón de parada
stop button

la rueda trasera
rear wheel

el billete de autobús
bus ticket

el timbre
bell

la estación de autobuses
bus station

la parada de autobús
bus stop

vocabulario • vocabulary

la tarifa	la marquesina
fare	bus shelter
el horario	la rampa para sillas de ruedas
timetable	wheelchair access

¿Para usted en…?	¿Qué autobús va a…?
Do you stop at…?	Which bus goes to…?

el microbús
minibus

el autobús turístico | tourist bus

el autobús de enlace | shuttle bus

el coche 1 • car 1

el exterior • exterior

el espejo retrovisor
rear view mirror

el limpiaparabrisas
windscreen wiper

la puerta
door

el retrovisor exterior
wing mirror

el parabrisas
windscreen

el maletero
boot

el capó
bonnet

el intermitente
indicator

la matrícula
licence plate

el parachoques
bumper

el faro
headlight

la rueda
wheel

el neumático
tyre

el equipaje
luggage

la baca
roofrack

la puerta del maletero
tailgate

el cinturón de seguridad
seat belt

la silla para niños
child seat

los modelos • types

el coche eléctrico
electric car

el coche de cinco puertas
hatchback

el turismo
saloon

el coche ranchera
estate

el coche descapotable
convertible

el coche deportivo
sports car

el monovolumen
people carrier

el todoterreno
four-wheel drive

el coche de época
vintage

la limousine
limousine

la gasolinera • petrol station

el surtidor
petrol pump

el precio
price

la zona de abastecimiento
forecourt

vocabulario • vocabulary

la gasolina petrol	**con plomo** leaded	**el lavadero de coches** car wash
el aceite oil	**el diesel** diesel	**el anticongelante** antifreeze
sin plomo unleaded	**el taller** garage	**el líquido limpiaparabrisas** screenwash

Lleno por favor.
Fill the tank, please.

el coche 2 · car 2

el interior · interior

el reposacabezas
headrest

el pestillo
door lock

el tirador
handle

el asiento trasero
back seat

el reposabrazos
armrest

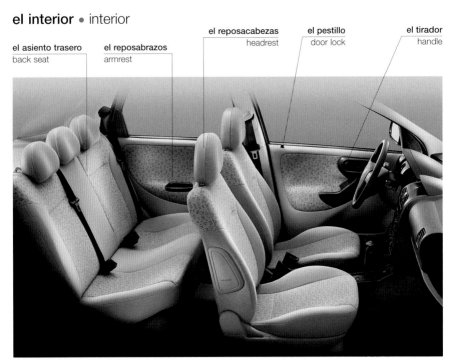

vocabulario · vocabulary

deportivo	**de cuatro puertas**	**automático**	**el freno**	**el acelerador**
two-door	four-door	automatic	brake	accelerator
de tres puertas	**manual**	**el encendido**	**el embrague**	**el aire acondicionado**
three-door	manual	ignition	clutch	air conditioning

¿Me puede decir cómo se va a...?
Can you tell me the way to...?

¿Dónde hay un parking?
Where is the car park?

¿Se puede aparcar aquí?
Can I park here?

los controles • controls

el volante
steering wheel

la bocina
horn

el salpicadero
dashboard

las luces de
emergencia
hazard lights

la navegación por satélite
satellite navigation

el volante a la izquierda | left-hand drive

el indicador de
temperatura
temperature gauge

el cuentarrevoluciones
rev counter

el indicador
de velocidad
speedometer

el indicador de la
gasolina
fuel gauge

el conmutador de
luces
lights switch

la radio del coche
car stereo

los mandos de la
calefacción
heater controls

la palanca de cambios
gearstick

el cuentakiló-
metros
odometer

el airbag
air bag

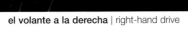

el volante a la derecha | right-hand drive

el coche 3 • car 3

la mecánica • mechanics

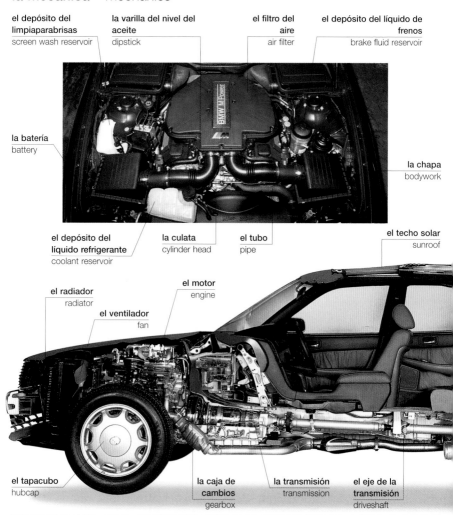

el depósito del limpiaparabrisas
screen wash reservoir

la varilla del nivel del aceite
dipstick

el filtro del aire
air filter

el depósito del líquido de frenos
brake fluid reservoir

la batería
battery

la chapa
bodywork

el depósito del líquido refrigerante
coolant reservoir

la culata
cylinder head

el tubo
pipe

el techo solar
sunroof

el radiador
radiator

el motor
engine

el ventilador
fan

el tapacubo
hubcap

la caja de cambios
gearbox

la transmisión
transmission

el eje de la transmisión
driveshaft

el pinchazo • puncture

la rueda de repuesto
spare tyre

la llave
wrench

los tornillos de la rueda
wheel nuts

el gato
jack

cambiar una rueda
change a wheel (v)

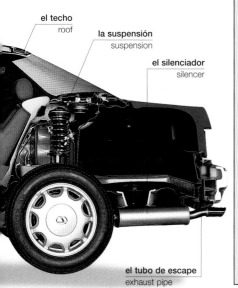

el techo
roof

la suspensión
suspension

el silenciador
silencer

el tubo de escape
exhaust pipe

---

vocabulario • vocabulary

el accidente de coche
car accident

la avería
breakdown

el seguro
insurance

la grúa
tow truck

el mecánico
mechanic

la caja de fusibles
fuse box

la bujía
spark plug

la presión del neumático
tyre pressure

la correa del ventilador
fan belt

el tanque de la gasolina
petrol tank

la correa del disco
cam belt

el turbo
turbocharger

el distribuidor
distributor

el ralentí
timing

el chasis
chassis

el freno de mano
handbrake

el alternador
alternator

....

Mi coche se ha averiado.
I've broken down.

Mi coche no arranca.
My car won't start.

la motocicleta • motorbike

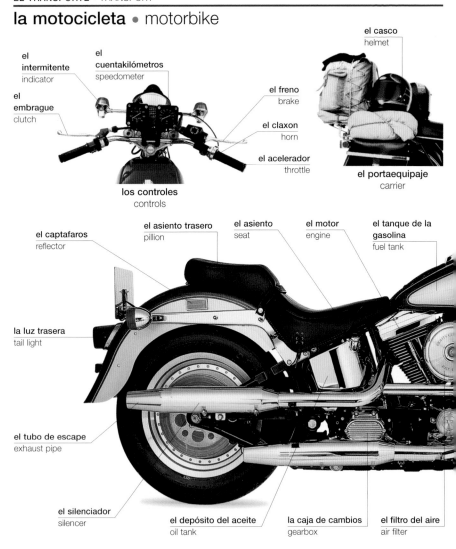

el casco
helmet

el intermitente
indicator

el cuentakilómetros
speedometer

el embrague
clutch

el freno
brake

el claxon
horn

el acelerador
throttle

el portaequipaje
carrier

los controles
controls

el captafaros
reflector

el asiento trasero
pillion

el asiento
seat

el motor
engine

el tanque de la gasolina
fuel tank

la luz trasera
tail light

el tubo de escape
exhaust pipe

el silenciador
silencer

el depósito del aceite
oil tank

la caja de cambios
gearbox

el filtro del aire
air filter

los tipos • types

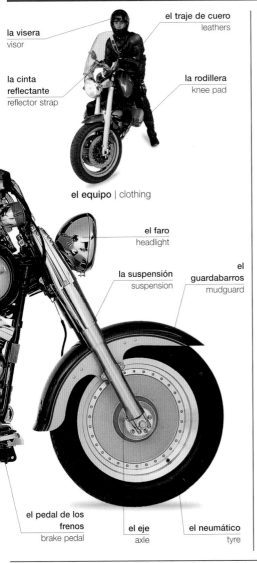

la visera
visor

el traje de cuero
leathers

la cinta
reflectante
reflector strap

la rodillera
knee pad

el equipo | clothing

la moto de carreras | racing bike

el parabrisas
windshield

el faro
headlight

la suspensión
suspension

el
guardabarros
mudguard

la moto de carretera | tourer

la moto de cross | dirt bike

el soporte
stand

el pedal de los
frenos
brake pedal

el eje
axle

el neumático
tyre

la vespa | scooter

la bicicleta • bicycle

el tándem
tandem

la bicicleta de
carreras
racing bike

la bicicleta de
montaña
mountain bike

la bicicleta de paseo
touring bike

la bicicleta de carretera
road bike

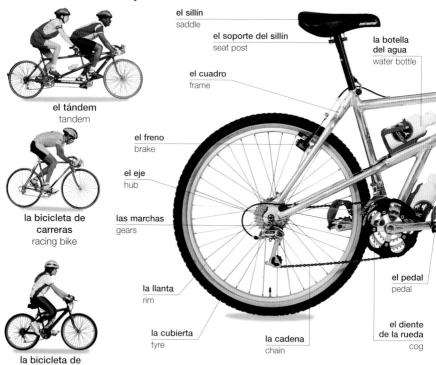

el sillín
saddle

el soporte del sillín
seat post

la botella
del agua
water bottle

el cuadro
frame

el freno
brake

el eje
hub

las marchas
gears

la llanta
rim

la cubierta
tyre

la cadena
chain

el pedal
pedal

el diente
de la rueda
cog

el casco
helmet

el carril de bicicletas | cycle lane

el tubo superior
crossbar

el manillar
handlebar

la palanca de cambio
gear lever

la palanca de frenos
brake lever

la palanca de la llanta
tyre lever

el parche
patch

el kit de reparaciones | repair kit

la horquilla
fork

la llave
key

el radio
spoke

la bomba
pump

el candado
lock

la rueda
wheel

la cámara
inner tube

la silla para el niño
child seat

la válvula
valve

la banda de rodadura
tread

---

vocabulario • vocabulary

el faro lamp	**la cesta** basket	**el cable** cable	**la dinamo** dynamo	**el calzapié** toe clip	**frenar** brake (v)
el faro trasero rear light	**la patilla de apoyo** kickstand	**el taco del freno** brake block	**la baca para bicicletas** bike rack	**la correa del calzapié** toe strap	**cambiar de marcha** change gear (v)
el captafaros reflector	**las ruedas de apoyo** stabilisers	**el piñón** sprocket	**el pinchazo** puncture	**pedalear** pedal (v)	**ir en bicicleta** cycle (v)

el tren • train

el vagón
carriage

el andén
platform

el carrito
trolley

el número de
andén
platform number

el viajero
de cercanías
commuter

la estación de tren | train station

los tipos de tren • types of train

la locomotora
engine

la cabina del
conductor
driver's cab

el raíl
rail

el tren de vapor
steam train

el tren diesel | diesel train

el tren eléctrico
electric train

el tren de alta velocidad
high-speed train

el monorraíl
monorail

el metro
underground train

el tranvía
tram

el tren de mercancías
freight train

el portaequipajes
luggage rack

la ventanilla
window

la puerta
door

el vagón
compartment

la vía
track

la barrera
ticket barrier

el asiento
seat

el sistema de megafonía
public address system

el horario
timetable

el billete
ticket

el vagón restaurante | dining car

el vestíbulo | concourse

el cochecama
sleeping compartment

vocabulario • vocabulary

la red ferroviaria rail network	**el plano del metro** underground map	**la taquilla** ticket office	**el raíl electrificado** live rail
el tren intercity inter-city train	**el retraso** delay	**el revisor** ticket inspector	**la señal** signal
la hora punta rush hour	**el precio** fare	**cambiar** change (v)	**la palanca de emergencia** emergency lever

el avión • aircraft

el avión de pasajeros • airliner

el fuselaje
fuselage

el ala
wing

la cola
tail

el morro
nose

la cabina
de pilotaje
cockpit

el motor
engine

el timón
rudder

la salida
exit

el tren
delantero
nosewheel

el tren de aterrizaje
landing gear

el alerón
aileron

la aleta
fin

el estabilizador
tailplane

la cabina • cabin

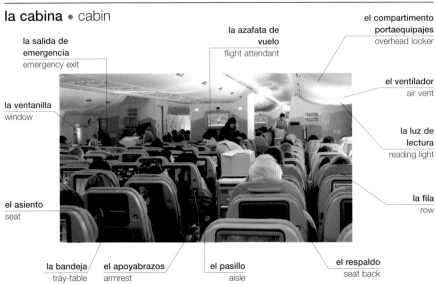

la azafata de
vuelo
flight attendant

el compartimento
portaequipajes
overhead locker

la salida de
emergencia
emergency exit

el ventilador
air vent

la ventanilla
window

la luz de
lectura
reading light

el asiento
seat

la fila
row

la bandeja
tray-table

el apoyabrazos
armrest

el pasillo
aisle

el respaldo
seat back

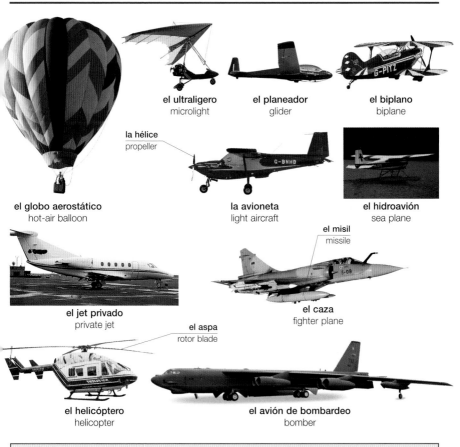

el ultraligero
microlight

el planeador
glider

el biplano
biplane

la hélice
propeller

el globo aerostático
hot-air balloon

la avioneta
light aircraft

el hidroavión
sea plane

el misil
missile

el jet privado
private jet

el caza
fighter plane

el aspa
rotor blade

el helicóptero
helicopter

el avión de bombardeo
bomber

vocabulario • vocabulary				
el piloto pilot	**despegar** take off (v)	**aterrizar** land (v)	**la clase turista** economy class	**el equipaje de mano** hand luggage
el copiloto co-pilot	**volar** fly (v)	**la altitud** altitude	**la clase preferente** business class	**el cinturón de seguridad** seat belt

el aeropuerto • airport

la pista de estacionamiento
apron

el remolque del equipaje
baggage trailer

la terminal
terminal

el vehículo de servicio
service vehicle

la pasarela
walkway

el avión de línea | airliner

vocabulario • vocabulary

la pista runway	**el número de vuelo** flight number	**la cinta de equipajes** carousel	**las vacaciones** holiday
el vuelo nacional domestic flight	**inmigración** immigration	**la seguridad** security	**reservar un vuelo** book a flight (v)
la conexión connection	**la aduana** customs	**la máquina de rayos x** X-ray machine	**facturar** check in (v)
el vuelo internacional international flight	**el exceso de equipaje** excess baggage	**el folleto de viajes** holiday brochure	**la torre de control** control tower

el equipaje de mano
hand luggage

el equipaje
luggage

el carro
trolley

el mostrador de facturación
check-in desk

el visado
visa

el pasaporte | passport

el control de pasaportes
passport control

la tarjeta de embarque
boarding pass

el billete
ticket

el número de puerta de embarque
gate number

las salidas
departures

la sala de embarque
departure lounge

el destino
destination

las llegadas
arrivals

la pantalla de información
information screen

la tienda libre de impuestos
duty-free shop

la recogida de equipajes
baggage reclaim

la parada de taxis
taxi rank

el alquiler de coches
car hire

el barco · ship

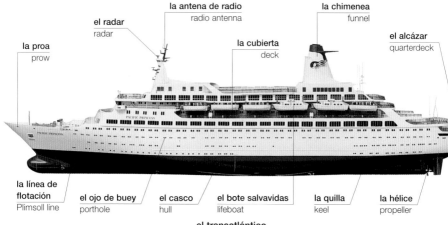

la antena de radio
radio antenna

el radar
radar

la chimenea
funnel

la proa
prow

la cubierta
deck

el alcázar
quarterdeck

la línea de
flotación
Plimsoll line

el ojo de buey
porthole

el casco
hull

el bote salvavidas
lifeboat

la quilla
keel

la hélice
propeller

el transatlántico
ocean liner

el puente
bridge

la sala de máquinas
engine room

el camarote
cabin

la cocina
galley

vocabulario · vocabulary

el muelle
dock

el cabrestante
windlass

el puerto
port

el capitán
captain

la pasarela
gangway

la lancha motora
speedboat

el ancla
anchor

la barca de remos
rowing boat

el noray
bollard

la piragua
canoe

otras embarcaciones • other ships

el ferry
ferry

el motor fueraborda
outboard motor

la zodiac
inflatable dinghy

el hidrodeslizador
hydrofoil

el yate
yacht

el catamarán
catamaran

el remolcador
tug boat

el aerodeslizador
hovercraft

el buque portacontenedores
container ship

las jarcias
rigging

la bodega
hold

el barco de vela
sailboat

el buque de carga
freighter

el petrolero
oil tanker

el portaviones
aircraft carrier

el barco de guerra
battleship

la falsa torre
conning tower

el submarino
submarine

el puerto • port

el almacén
warehouse

la grúa
crane

la carretilla elevadora
fork-lift truck

la carretera de acceso
access road

las aduanas
del puerto
customs house

la dársena
dock

el contenedor
container

el muelle
quay

la carga
cargo

la terminal del ferry
ferry terminal

el ferry
ferry

la ventanilla
de pasajes
ticket office

el pasajero
passenger

el muelle comercial | container port

el muelle de pasajeros | passenger port

la red
net

el barco de pesca
fishing boat

el punto de amarre
mooring

el puerto deportivo
marina

el puerto de pesca
fishing port

el puerto
harbour

el embarcadero
pier

el espigón
jetty

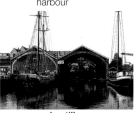

el astillero
shipyard

la lámpara
lamp

el faro
lighthouse

la boya
buoy

---

vocabulario • vocabulary

el guardacostas coastguard	**el dique seco** dry dock	**embarcar** board (v)
el capitán del puerto harbour master	**amarrar** moor (v)	**desembarcar** disembark (v)
fondear drop anchor (v)	**atracar** dock (v)	**zarpar** set sail (v)

los deportes
sports

el fútbol americano • American football

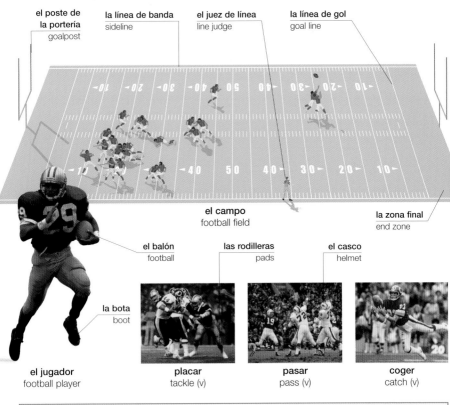

el poste de
la portería
goalpost

la línea de banda
sideline

el juez de línea
line judge

la línea de gol
goal line

el campo
football field

la zona final
end zone

el balón
football

las rodilleras
pads

el casco
helmet

la bota
boot

el jugador
football player

placar
tackle (v)

pasar
pass (v)

coger
catch (v)

vocabulario • vocabulary

el tiempo muerto time out	**el equipo** team	**la defensa** defence	**la animadora** cheerleader	**¿Cómo van?** What is the score?
el mal pase de balón fumble	**el ataque** attack	**la puntuación** score	**el ensayo** touchdown	**¿Quién va ganando?** Who is winning?

el rugby • rugby

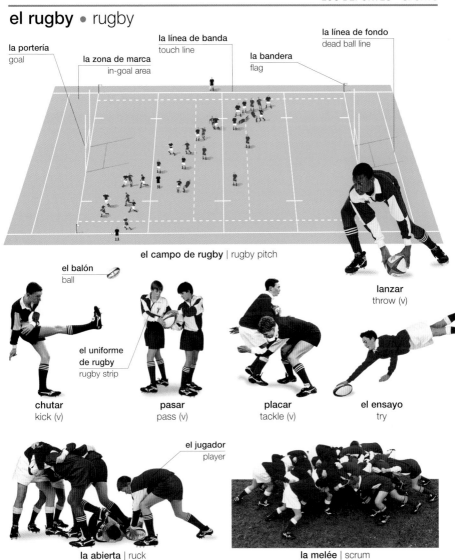

la portería
goal

la zona de marca
in-goal area

la línea de banda
touch line

la bandera
flag

la línea de fondo
dead ball line

el campo de rugby | rugby pitch

el balón
ball

el uniforme
de rugby
rugby strip

lanzar
throw (v)

chutar
kick (v)

pasar
pass (v)

placar
tackle (v)

el ensayo
try

el jugador
player

la abierta | ruck

la melée | scrum

el fútbol • soccer

el balón
football

el delantero
forward

el árbitro
referee

el círculo central
centre circle

el portero
goalkeeper

el uniforme
football strip

el futbolista
footballer

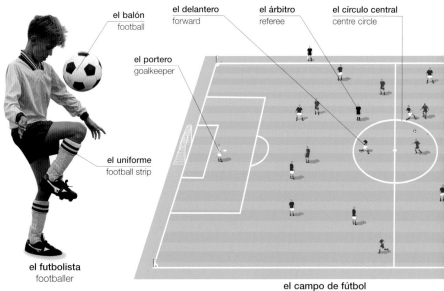

el campo de fútbol
football pitch

el poste
goalpost

la red
net

el larguero
crossbar

el gol | goal

regatear | dribble (v)

tirar de cabeza
head (v)

la barrera
wall

el tiro libre | free kick

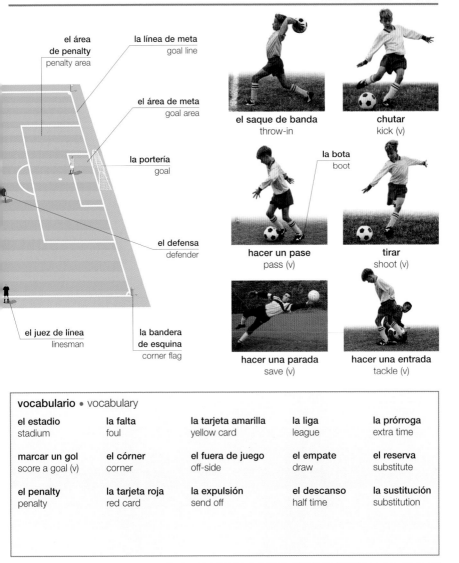

el área de penalty
penalty area

la línea de meta
goal line

el área de meta
goal area

la portería
goal

el defensa
defender

el juez de línea
linesman

la bandera de esquina
corner flag

el saque de banda
throw-in

chutar
kick (v)

la bota
boot

hacer un pase
pass (v)

tirar
shoot (v)

hacer una parada
save (v)

hacer una entrada
tackle (v)

vocabulario • vocabulary

el estadio stadium	**la falta** foul	**la tarjeta amarilla** yellow card	**la liga** league	**la prórroga** extra time
marcar un gol score a goal (v)	**el córner** corner	**el fuera de juego** off-side	**el empate** draw	**el reserva** substitute
el penalty penalty	**la tarjeta roja** red card	**la expulsión** send off	**el descanso** half time	**la sustitución** substitution

el hockey • hockey

el hockey sobre hielo • ice hockey

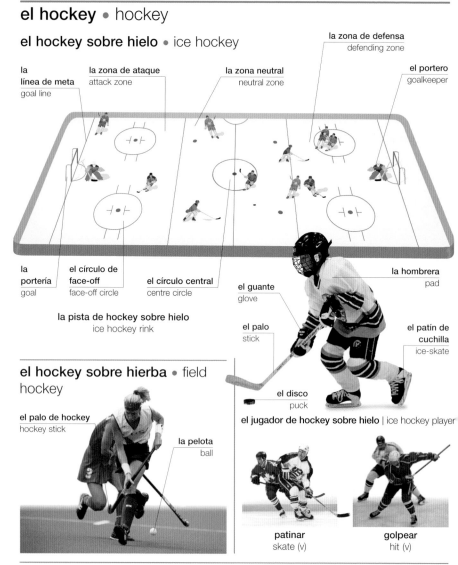

la línea de meta
goal line

la zona de ataque
attack zone

la zona neutral
neutral zone

la zona de defensa
defending zone

el portero
goalkeeper

la portería
goal

el círculo de face-off
face-off circle

el círculo central
centre circle

la pista de hockey sobre hielo
ice hockey rink

el guante
glove

el palo
stick

el disco
puck

la hombrera
pad

el patín de cuchilla
ice-skate

el jugador de hockey sobre hielo | ice hockey player

el hockey sobre hierba • field hockey

el palo de hockey
hockey stick

la pelota
ball

patinar
skate (v)

golpear
hit (v)

el críquet • cricket

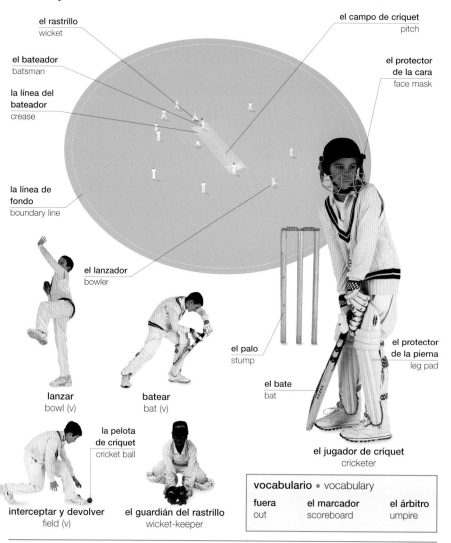

el rastrillo
wicket

el campo de críquet
pitch

el bateador
batsman

el protector
de la cara
face mask

la línea del
bateador
crease

la línea de
fondo
boundary line

el lanzador
bowler

el palo
stump

el protector
de la pierna
leg pad

el bate
bat

lanzar
bowl (v)

batear
bat (v)

la pelota
de críquet
cricket ball

el jugador de críquet
cricketer

interceptar y devolver
field (v)

el guardián del rastrillo
wicket-keeper

vocabulario • vocabulary		
fuera	el marcador	el árbitro
out	scoreboard	umpire

el baloncesto • basketball

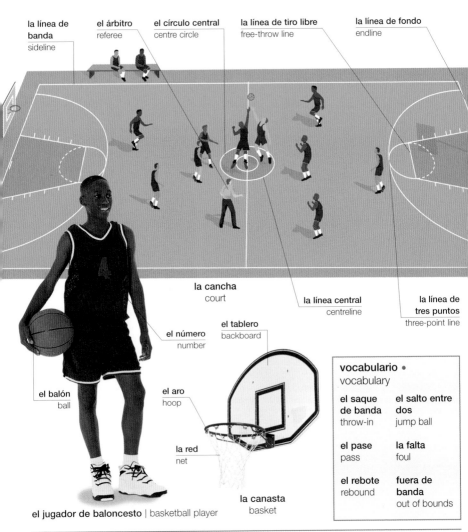

la línea de banda
sideline

el árbitro
referee

el círculo central
centre circle

la línea de tiro libre
free-throw line

la línea de fondo
endline

la cancha
court

la línea central
centreline

la línea de tres puntos
three-point line

el número
number

el tablero
backboard

el balón
ball

el aro
hoop

la red
net

la canasta
basket

el jugador de baloncesto | basketball player

---

vocabulario •
vocabulary

el saque de banda throw-in	**el salto entre dos** jump ball
el pase pass	**la falta** foul
el rebote rebound	**fuera de banda** out of bounds

las acciones • actions

lanzar
throw (v)

coger
catch (v)

tirar
shoot (v)

saltar
jump (v)

marcar
mark (v)

bloquear
block (v)

botar
bounce (v)

marcar
dunk (v)

el balonvolea • volleyball

bloquear
block (v)

la red
net

recibir
dig (v)

el árbitro
referee

la rodillera
knee support

la cancha | court

el béisbol • baseball

el campo • field

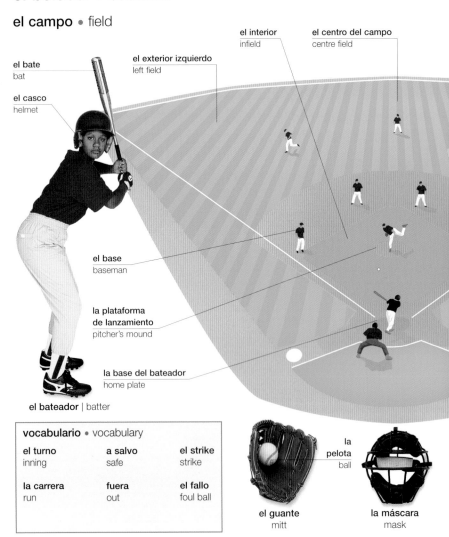

el bate
bat

el casco
helmet

el exterior izquierdo
left field

el interior
infield

el centro del campo
centre field

el base
baseman

**la plataforma
de lanzamiento**
pitcher's mound

la base del bateador
home plate

el bateador | batter

vocabulario • vocabulary

el turno	**a salvo**	**el strike**
inning	safe	strike
la carrera	**fuera**	**el fallo**
run	out	foul ball

la pelota
ball

el guante
mitt

la máscara
mask

las acciones • actions

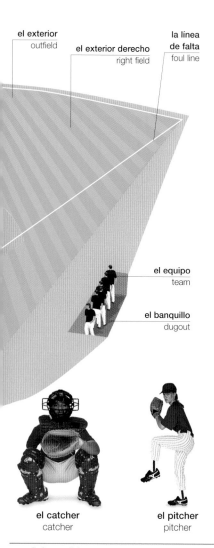

el exterior
outfield

el exterior derecho
right field

la línea
de falta
foul line

el equipo
team

el banquillo
dugout

el catcher
catcher

el pitcher
pitcher

lanzar | throw (v)

coger | catch (v)

correr
run (v)

defender
field (v)

resbalar
slide (v)

perseguir
tag (v)

lanzar
pitch (v)

batear
bat (v)

el árbitro
umpire

jugar | play (v)

el tenis • tennis

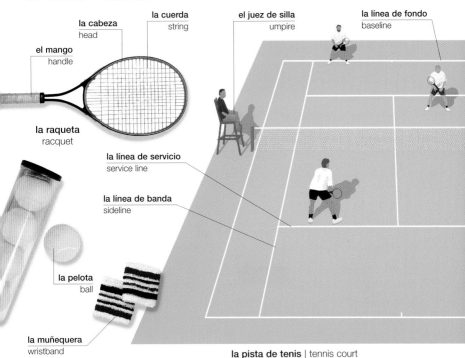

la cabeza / head

la cuerda / string

el mango / handle

la raqueta / racquet

la línea de servicio / service line

la línea de banda / sideline

la pelota / ball

la muñequera / wristband

el juez de silla / umpire

la línea de fondo / baseline

la pista de tenis | tennis court

vocabulario • vocabulary

el individual singles	**el set** set	**nada** love	**la falta** fault	**el peloteo** rally	**el efecto** spin
los dobles doubles	**el partido** match	**la ventaja** advantage	**el ace** ace	**¡red!** let!	**el juez de línea** linesman
el juego game	**el tiebreak** tiebreak	**cuarenta iguales** deuce	**la dejada** dropshot	**el tiro con efecto** slice	**el campeonato** championship

los golpes • strokes

la red
net

el mate
smash

el recogepelotas
ballboy

sacar
serve (v)

los tenis
tennis shoes

el jugador
player

el servicio
serve

la volea
volley

le resto
return

el globo
lob

el derecho
forehand

el revés
backhand

los juegos de raqueta • racquet games

el volante
shuttlecock

la pala
bat

el bádminton
badminton

el ping-pong
table tennis

el squash
squash

el racketball
racquetball

el golf • golf

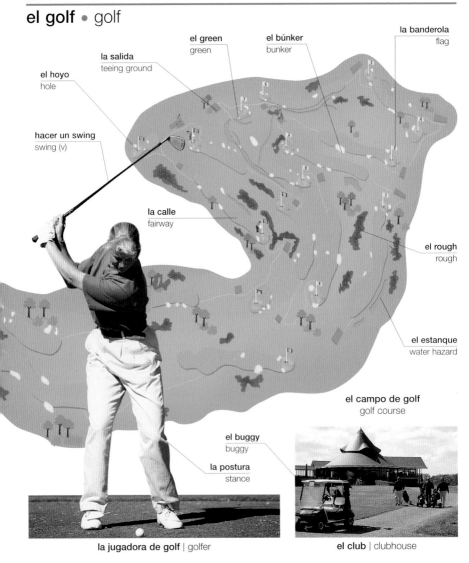

el green
green

el búnker
bunker

la banderola
flag

la salida
teeing ground

el hoyo
hole

hacer un swing
swing (v)

la calle
fairway

el rough
rough

el estanque
water hazard

el campo de golf
golf course

el buggy
buggy

la postura
stance

la jugadora de golf | golfer

el club | clubhouse

el equipo • equipment

los palos de golf • golf clubs

la pelota de golf
golf ball

el paraguas
umbrella

la bolsa de golf
golf bag

el tee
tee

los clavos
spikes

el palo de madera
wood

el guante
glove

el carrito de golf
golf trolley

el zapato de golf
golf shoe

el putter
putter

las acciones • actions

salir
tee-off (v)

hacer un drive
drive (v)

tirar al hoyo con un putter
putt (v)

hacer un chip
chip (v)

el palo de hierro
iron

el wedge
wedge

vocabulario • vocabulary

el par par	el sobre par over par	el handicap handicap	el caddy caddy	el golpe stroke	el backswing backswing
el bajo par under par	el hoyo en uno hole in one	el torneo tournament	los espectadores spectators	el swing de práctica practice swing	la línea de juego line of play

el atletismo • athletics

la calle
lane

la pista
track

la línea de meta
finishing line

la línea de salida
starting line

el campo
field

la atleta
athlete

el cajón
de salida
starting
blocks

el esprinter
sprinter

el lanzamiento
de disco
discus

el lanzamiento de
peso
shotput

el lanzamiento de jabalina
javelin

vocabulario • vocabulary

la carrera race	el récord record	la fotofinish photo finish	el salto con pértiga pole vault
el tiempo time	batir un récord break a record (v)	la maratón marathon	la marca personal personal best

el cronómetro
stopwatch

el testigo
baton

el listón
crossbar

la carrera de relevos
relay race

el salto de altura
high jump

el salto de longitud
long jump

la carrera de vallas
hurdles

la gimnasia • gymnastics

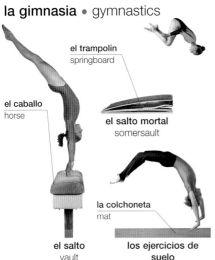

el trampolín
springboard

la gimnasta
gymnast

el caballo
horse

el salto mortal
somersault

la barra de equilibrio
beam

la cinta
ribbon

la colchoneta
mat

el salto
vault

**los ejercicios de
suelo**
floor exercises

la voltereta
tumble

la gimnasia rítmica
rhythmic gymnastics

vocabulario • vocabulary

la barra fija horizontal bar	**las paralelas asimétricas** asymmetric bars	**las anillas** rings	**las medallas** medals	**la plata** silver
las paralelas parallel bars	**el caballo con arcos** pommel horse	**el podio** podium	**el oro** gold	**el bronce** bronze

los deportes de combate • combat sports

el adversario
opponent

el protector
guard

el guante
glove

el cinturón
belt

el taekwondo
tae-kwon-do

el karate
karate

el judo
judo

la careta
mask

la espada
sword

el kendo
kendo

el aikido
aikido

el kung fu
kung fu

el full contact
kickboxing

la lucha libre
wrestling

el boxeo
boxing

los movimientos • actions

la caída
fall

el agarre
hold

el derribo
throw

la inmovilización
pin

la patada
kick

el puñetazo
punch

el golpe
strike

el salto
jump

la parada
block

el golpe
chop

vocabulario • vocabulary

el ring
boxing ring

el asalto
round

el puño
fist

el cinturón negro
black belt

la capoeira
capoeira

el protegedientes
mouth guard

el combate
bout

el K.O.
knock out

las artes marciales
martial arts

el sumo
sumo wrestling

los guantes de boxeo
boxing gloves

el entrenamiento
sparring

el saco de arena
punch bag

la defensa personal
self defence

el tai-chi
tai-chi

la natación • swimming
el equipo • equipment

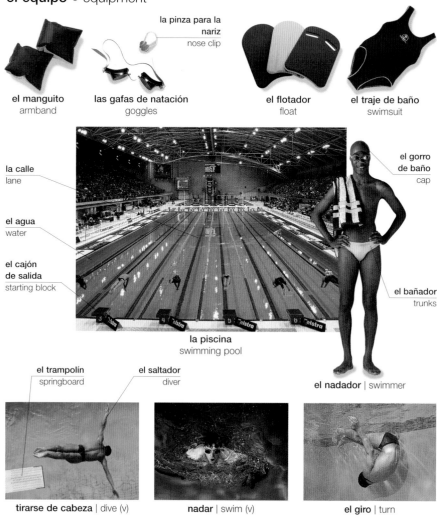

la pinza para la nariz
nose clip

el manguito
armband

las gafas de natación
goggles

el flotador
float

el traje de baño
swimsuit

la calle
lane

el gorro de baño
cap

el agua
water

el cajón de salida
starting block

el bañador
trunks

la piscina
swimming pool

el nadador | swimmer

el trampolín
springboard

el saltador
diver

tirarse de cabeza | dive (v)

nadar | swim (v)

el giro | turn

los estilos • styles

el crol
front crawl

la braza
breaststroke

la brazada
stroke

la patada
kick

la espalda | backstroke

la mariposa | butterfly

el buceo • scuba diving

el traje de buzo
wetsuit

la botella de aire
air cylinder

la aleta
flipper

las gafas
mask

el regulador
regulator

el cinturón
de pesas
weight belt

el tubo
snorkel

---

vocabulario • vocabulary

el salto dive	**hacer agua** tread water (v)	**las taquillas** lockers	**el waterpolo** water polo	**la zona poco profunda** shallow end	**el tirón** cramp
el salto alto high dive	**el salto de salida** racing dive	**el socorrista** lifeguard	**la zona profunda** deep end	**la natación sincronizada** synchronized swimming	**ahogarse** drown (v)

la vela • sailing

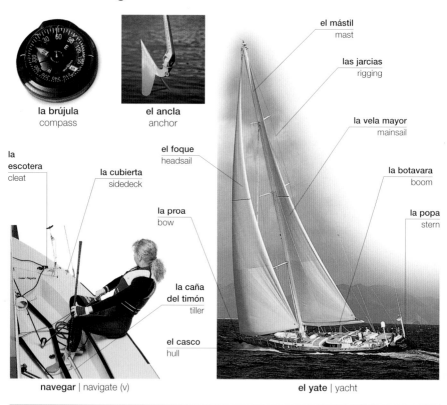

la brújula
compass

el ancla
anchor

el mástil
mast

las jarcias
rigging

la vela mayor
mainsail

el foque
headsail

la
escotera
cleat

la cubierta
sidedeck

la botavara
boom

la popa
stern

la proa
bow

la caña
del timón
tiller

el casco
hull

navegar | navigate (v)

el yate | yacht

la seguridad • safety

la bengala
flare

el salvavidas
lifebuoy

el chaleco salvavidas
life jacket

la balsa salvavidas
life raft

los deportes acuáticos • watersports

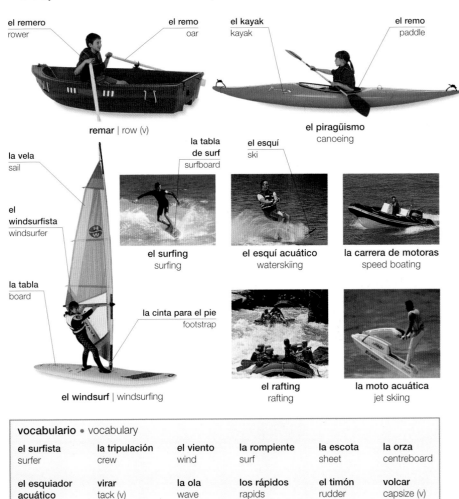

el remero
rower

el remo
oar

el kayak
kayak

el remo
paddle

remar | row (v)

el piragüismo
canoeing

la vela
sail

la tabla
de surf
surfboard

el esquí
ski

el
windsurfista
windsurfer

el surfing
surfing

el esquí acuático
waterskiing

la carrera de motoras
speed boating

la tabla
board

la cinta para el pie
footstrap

el rafting
rafting

la moto acuática
jet skiing

el windsurf | windsurfing

vocabulario • vocabulary

el surfista surfer	**la tripulación** crew	**el viento** wind	**la rompiente** surf	**la escota** sheet	**la orza** centreboard
el esquiador acuático waterskier	**virar** tack (v)	**la ola** wave	**los rápidos** rapids	**el timón** rudder	**volcar** capsize (v)

la equitación • horse riding

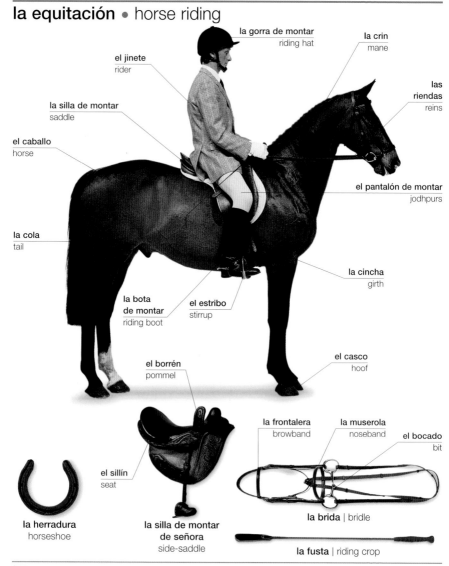

la gorra de montar
riding hat

la crin
mane

el jinete
rider

las riendas
reins

la silla de montar
saddle

el caballo
horse

el pantalón de montar
jodhpurs

la cola
tail

la cincha
girth

la bota de montar
riding boot

el estribo
stirrup

el casco
hoof

el borrén
pommel

la frontalera
browband

la muserola
noseband

el bocado
bit

el sillín
seat

la brida | bridle

la herradura
horseshoe

la silla de montar de señora
side-saddle

la fusta | riding crop

las modalidades • events

el caballo de carreras
racehorse

la valla
fence

la carrera de caballos
horse race

la carrera de obstáculos
steeplechase

la carrera al trote
harness race

el rodeo
rodeo

el concurso de saltos
showjumping

la carrera de carrozas
carriage race

el paseo
trekking

la doma y monta
dressage

el polo
polo

---

vocabulario • vocabulary

el paso walk	**el medio galope** canter	**el galope** gallop	**el cabestro** halter	**el cercado** paddock	**el hipódromo** racecourse
el trote trot	**el mozo de cuadra** groom	**el salto** jump	**la cuadra** stable	**el ruedo** arena	**la carrera sin obstáculos** flat race

---

la pesca • fishing

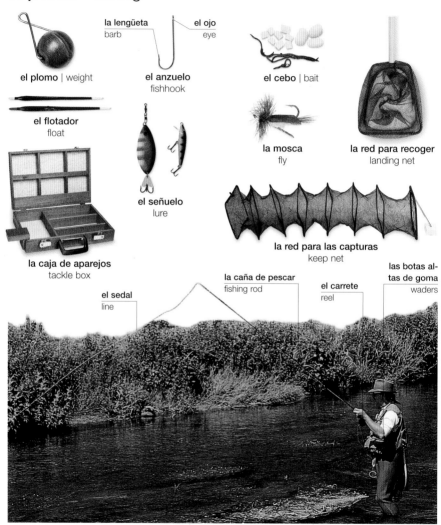

el plomo | weight

la lengüeta barb

el ojo eye

el anzuelo fishhook

el cebo | bait

el flotador float

el señuelo lure

la mosca fly

la red para recoger landing net

la caja de aparejos tackle box

la red para las capturas keep net

el sedal line

la caña de pescar fishing rod

el carrete reel

las botas altas de goma waders

el pescador de caña | angler

los tipos de pesca • types of fishing

la pesca en agua dulce
freshwater fishing

la pesca con mosca
fly fishing

la pesca deportiva
sport fishing

la pesca de altura
deep sea fishing

la pesca en la orilla
surfcasting

las acciones • activities

lanzar	coger	recoger	coger con la red	soltar
cast (v)	catch (v)	reel in (v)	net (v)	release (v)

---

vocabulario • vocabulary

cebar	**los aparejos**	**la ropa impermeable**	**la licencia de pesca**	**la nasa**
bait (v)	tackle	waterproofs	fishing permit	creel
picar	**el carrete**	**la pértiga**	**la pesca en alta mar**	**la pesca con arpón**
bite (v)	spool	pole	marine fishing	spearfishing

el esquí • skiing

la pista
ski slope

la telesilla
chairlift

el teleférico
cable car

el guante
glove

el bastón
ski pole

la pista de esquí
ski run

la barrera de seguridad
safety barrier

la punta
tip

el canto
edge

el esquí
ski

la chaqueta de esquí
ski jacket

la esquiadora
skier

la bota de esquí
ski boot

las modalidades • events

el descenso
downhill skiing

el poste
gate

el slálom
slalom

el salto
ski jump

el esquí de fondo
cross-country skiing

los deportes de invierno • winter sports

la escalada en hielo
ice climbing

el patinaje sobre hielo
ice-skating

las gafas
goggles

el patín
skate

el patinaje artístico
figure skating

el snowboarding
snowboarding

el bobsleigh
bobsleigh

el luge
luge

vocabulario • vocabulary

el esquí alpino
alpine skiing

el trineo con perros
dog sledding

el slálom gigante
giant slalom

el biatlón
biathlon

fuera de pista
off-piste

la avalancha
avalanche

el curling
curling

el patinaje de velocidad
speed skating

la moto de nieve
snowmobile

tirarse en trineo
sledding

los otros deportes • other sports

el planeador
glider

el ala delta
hang-glider

el vuelo sin motor
gliding

el paracaídas
parachute

el vuelo con ala delta
hang-gliding

la cuerda
rope

la escalada
rock climbing

el paracaidismo
parachuting

el parapente
paragliding

el paracaidismo en caída libre
skydiving

el rappel
abseiling

el puenting
bungee jumping

el piloto de carreras
racing driver

el rally
rally driving

el automovilismo
motor racing

el motocross
motorcross

el motociclismo
motorbike racing

el monopatín
skateboard

el palo
stick

la máscara
mask

el florete
foil

montar en monopatín
skateboarding

el patinaje en línea
inline skating

el lacrosse
lacrosse

el esgrima
fencing

el bolo
pin

el arco
bow

la diana
target

la flecha
arrow

el carcaj
quiver

el tiro con arco
archery

el tiro
target shooting

la bola de bowling
bowling ball

los bolos
bowling

el billar americano
pool

el billar
snooker

la forma física • fitness

la bicicleta fija
exercise bike

la máquina de
ejercicios
gym machine

el banco
bench

las pesas
free weights

la barra
bar

el gimasio
gym

la máquina de
remos
rowing machine

la banda de paseo
treadmill

la máquina de cross
cross trainer

la entrenadora
personal
personal trainer

la máquina de step
step machine

la piscina
swimming pool

la sauna
sauna

los ejercicios • exercises

el estiramiento
stretch

la flexión con estiramiento
lunge

los leotardos
tights

la flexión
press-up

ponerse en cuclillas
squat

el abdominal
sit-up

la pesa
dumb bell

el ejercicio de bíceps
bicep curl

los ejercicios de piernas
leg press

las zapatillas
trainers

la barra de pesas
weight bar

los ejercicios pectorales
chest press

el levantamiento de pesas
weight training

el footing
jogging

el pilates
pilates

---

vocabulario • vocabulary

entrenar train (v)	**correr en parada** jog on the spot (v)	**estirar** extend (v)	**la gimnasia prepugilística** boxercise	**saltar a la comba** skipping
calentar warm up (v)	**flexionar** flex (v)	**levantar** pull up (v)	**la tabla de gimnasia** circuit training	

el ocio
leisure

el teatro • theatre

el telón
curtain

los bastidores
wings

el decorado
set

el público
audience

la orquesta
orchestra

el escenario | stage

la butaca
seat

la platea alta
upper circle

la fila
row

el palco
box

la platea
circle

la galería
balcony

el pasillo
aisle

el patio de
butacas
stalls

las butacas | seating

vocabulario • vocabulary

la obra play	**el director** director	**el estreno** first night
el reparto cast	**el productor** producer	**el descanso** interval
el actor actor	**el guión** script	**el programa** programme
la actriz actress	**el telón de fondo** backdrop	**el foso de la orquesta** orchestra pit

el concierto
concert

el musical
musical

el traje
costume

el ballet
ballet

vocabulario • vocabulary

el acomodador
usher

la música clásica
classical music

la partitura
musical score

la banda sonora
soundtrack

aplaudir
applaud (v)

el bis
encore

Quisiera dos entradas para la sesión de esta noche.
I'd like two tickets for tonight's performance.

¿A qué hora empieza?
What time does it start?

la ópera
opera

el cine • cinema

las palomitas
popcorn

la taquilla
box office

el póster
poster

el vestíbulo
lobby

el cine
cinema hall

la pantalla
screen

vocabulario • vocabulary

la comedia
comedy

la película de suspense
thriller

la película de terror
horror film

la película del oeste
western

la película romántica
romance

la película de ciencia ficción
science fiction film

la película de aventuras
adventure

la película de dibujos animados
animated film

la orquesta • orchestra

la cuerda • strings

el arpa
harp

el director de orquesta
conductor

el contrabajo
double bass

el violín
violin

el podio
podium

la viola
viola

el violoncelo
cello

la partitura
score

la clave de sol
treble clef

la nota
note

el penta-grama
staff

la clave de fa
bass clef

Andante

el piano | piano

la notación | notation

vocabulario • vocabulary

la obertura overture	**la sonata** sonata	**la pausa** rest	**sostenido** sharp	**natural** natural	**la escala** scale
la sinfonía symphony	**los instrumentos** instruments	**el tono** pitch	**bemol** flat	**la barra** bar	**la batura** baton

el viento-madera • woodwind

el flautín
piccolo

la flauta
flute

el oboe
oboe

el corno inglés
cor anglais

el clarinete
clarinet

el clarinete bajo
bass clarinet

el fagote
bassoon

el contrafagote
double bassoon

el saxofón
saxophone

la percusión • percussion

el vibráfono
vibraphone

los bongos
bongos

el tambor pequeño
snare drum

el timbal
kettledrum

el gong
gong

el triángulo
triangle

las maracas
maracas

los platillos
cymbals

la pandereta
tambourine

el pedal
foot pedal

el viento-metal • brass

la trompeta
trumpet

el trombón de varas
trombone

el corno de caza
French horn

la tuba
tuba

el concierto • concert

el altavoz
speaker

los fans
fans

el cantante
lead singer

el guitarrista
guitarist

el micrófono
microphone

el batería
drummer

el concierto de rock | rock concert

los instrumentos • instruments

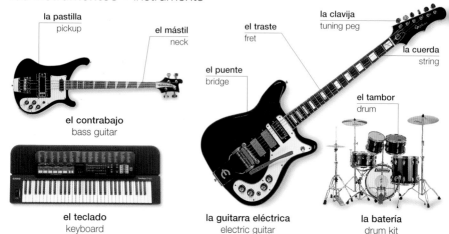

la pastilla
pickup

el mástil
neck

el contrabajo
bass guitar

el teclado
keyboard

el traste
fret

el puente
bridge

la clavija
tuning peg

la cuerda
string

el tambor
drum

la guitarra eléctrica
electric guitar

la batería
drum kit

los estilos musicales • musical styles

el jazz
jazz

el blues
blues

el punk
punk

la música folk
folk music

el pop
pop

la música de baile
dance

el rap
rap

el heavy metal
heavy metal

la música clásica
classical music

vocabulario • vocabulary						
la canción	**la letra**	**la melodía**	**el ritmo**	**el reggae**	**la música country**	**el foco**
song	lyrics	melody	beat	reggae	country	spotlight

el turismo • sightseeing

el itinerario
itinerary

descubierto
open-top

el turista
tourist

el autobús turístico | tour bus

la guía
turística
tour guide

la estatuilla
statuette

la visita con guía
guided tour

los recuerdos
souvenirs

la atracción turística | tourist attraction

---

vocabulario • vocabulary

el precio de entrada entrance fee	la guía del viajero guide book	la cámara de vídeo camcorder	la izquierda left	**¿Dónde está…?** Where is…?
abierto open	la película film	las indicaciones directions	la derecha right	**Me he perdido.** I'm lost.
cerrado closed	las pilas batteries	la máquina fotográfica camera	recto straight on	**¿Podría decirme cómo se va a…?** Can you tell me the way to….?

los lugares de interés • attractions

el cuadro
painting

la muestra
exhibit

la exposición
exhibition

la ruina famosa
famous ruin

el museo
art gallery

el monumento
monument

el museo
museum

el edificio histórico
historic building

el casino
casino

los jardines
gardens

el parque nacional
national park

la información • information

las horas
times

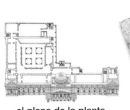

el plano de la planta
floor plan

el plano
map

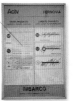

el horario
timetable

la oficina de información
tourist information

las actividades al aire libre • outdoor activities

el sendero
footpath

el reloj de sol
sundial

la cafetería
café

el parque | park

la hierba
grass

el banco
bench

los
jardines clásicos
formal gardens

la montaña rusa
roller coaster

la feria
fairground

**el parque de
atracciones**
theme park

el safari park
safari park

el zoo
zoo

las actividades • activites

el ciclismo
cycling

el footing
jogging

montar en patinete
skateboarding

el patinaje
rollerblading

el sendero para caballos
bridle path

la ornitología
bird watching

la equitación
horse riding

el senderismo
hiking

la cesta
hamper

el picnic
picnic

el área de juegos • playground

el cajón de arena
sandpit

la piscina de plástico
paddling pool

los columpios
swings

el subibaja | seesaw

el tobogán
slide

la estructura para escalar
climbing frame

la playa • beach

el hotel
hotel

la sombrilla
beach umbrella

la caseta
beach hut

la arena
sand

la ola
wave

el mar
sea

la bolsa de playa
beach bag

el bikini
bikini

tomar el sol | sunbathe (v)

el socorrista
lifeguard

la torre de vigilancia
lifeguard tower

la barrera contra el viento
windbreak

el paseo marítimo
promenade

la hamaca
deck chair

las gafas de sol
sunglasses

el sombrero para el sol
sunhat

la crema bronceadora
suntan lotion

la crema protectora
sunblock

la pelota de playa
beach ball

el flotador
rubber ring

el bañador
swimsuit

la pala
spade

el cubo
bucket

la toalla de playa
beach towel

el castillo de arena
sandcastle

la concha
shell

el camping • camping

los aseos
toilets

el contenedor de la basura
waste disposal

las duchas
shower block

el punto eléctrico
electric hook-up

el doble techo
flysheet

la clavija
tent peg

la cuerda
guy rope

la roulotte
caravan

el camping
campsite

---

vocabulario • vocabulary

acampar camp (v)	**la plaza** pitch	**la mesa de picnic** picnic bench	**el carbón vegetal** charcoal
la oficina del director site manager's office	**montar una tienda** pitch a tent (v)	**la hamaca** hammock	**la hoguera** campfire
hay plazas libres pitches available	**el palo de la tienda** tent pole	**la cámper** camper van	**la pastilla para hogueras** firelighter
completo full	**el catre de campaña** camp bed	**el remolque** trailer	**encender una hoguera** light a fire (v)

la estructura
frame

el suelo aislante
ground sheet

la mochila
backpack

el termo
vacuum flask

la cantimplora
water bottle

la tienda de campaña
tent

la loción contra los insectos
insect repellent

la linterna
torch

la mosquitera
mosquito net

la ropa termoaislante
thermals

las botas de trekking
walking boots

la ropa impermeable
waterproofs

el saco de dormir
sleeping bag

el hornillo
camping stove

la barbacoa
barbecue

la esterilla
sleeping mat

la colchoneta | air mattress

el ocio en el hogar • home entertainment

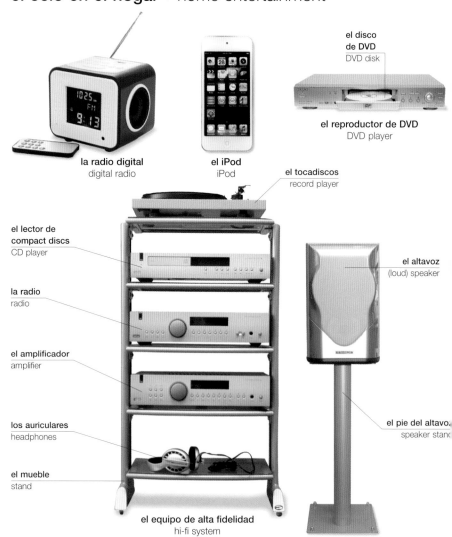

el disco de DVD
DVD disk

el reproductor de DVD
DVD player

la radio digital
digital radio

el iPod
iPod

el tocadiscos
record player

el lector de compact discs
CD player

el altavoz
(loud) speaker

la radio
radio

el amplificador
amplifier

los auriculares
headphones

el pie del altavoz
speaker stand

el mueble
stand

el equipo de alta fidelidad
hi-fi system

el sintonizador digital
digital box

la pantalla
screen

el borde del ocular
eyecup

la cámara de vídeo
camcorder

la antena parabólica
satellite dish

el televisor de pantalla plana
flatscreen TV

la consola
console

el avance rápido
fast forward

la pausa
pause

el botón para grabar
record

el volumen
volume

el botón para rebobinar
rewind

el play
play

el stop
stop

el mando a distancia
remote control

los controles
controller

el videojuego | video game

vocabulario • vocabulary

el compact disc compact disc	**estéreo** stereo	**el magnetofón** cassette player	**la Wi-Fi** wifi	**ver la televisión** watch television (v)
la casete cassette tape	**el anuncio** advertisement	**la televisión por cable** cable television	**el largometraje** feature film	**apagar la televisión** turn the television off (v)
el programa programme	**la transmisión por secuencias** streaming	**el canal de pay per view** pay per view channel	**cambiar de canal** change channel (v)	**sintonizar la radio** tune the radio (v)
digital digital	**alta definición** high-definition		**encender la televisión** turn the television on (v)	

la fotografía • photography

el disparador
shutter release

la rueda del diafragma
aperture dial

l'objectif
lens

la cámara réflex | SLR camera

el filtro
filter

la tapa del objetivo
lens cap

el flash electrónico
flash gun

el fotómetro
lightmeter

el teleobjetivo
zoom lens

el trípode
tripod

los tipos de cámara • types of camera

la cámara Polaroid
polaroid camera

el flash
flash

la cámara APS
APS camera

el teléfono con cámara
cameraphone

la cámara desechable
disposable camera

fotografiar • photograph (v)

el carrete
film spool

la película
film

enfocar
focus (v)

revelar
develop (v)

el negativo
negative

apaisado
landscape

en formato vertical
portrait

la fotografía | photograph

el álbum de fotos
photo album

el portarretratos
photo frame

los problemas • problems

subexpuesto
underexposed

sobreexpuesto
overexposed

desenfocado
out of focus

los ojos rojos
red eye

vocabulario • vocabulary

el visor viewfinder	**la foto (revelada)** print
la funda de la cámara camera case	**mate** mat
la exposición exposure	**con brillo** gloss
el cuarto oscuro darkroom	**la ampliación** enlargement

Me gustaría revelar este carrete.
I'd like this film processed

los juegos • games

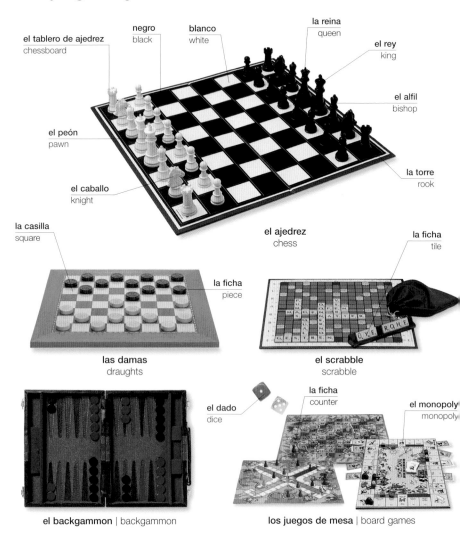

el tablero de ajedrez
chessboard

negro
black

blanco
white

la reina
queen

el rey
king

el alfil
bishop

el peón
pawn

el caballo
knight

la torre
rook

la casilla
square

el ajedrez
chess

la ficha
tile

la ficha
piece

las damas
draughts

el scrabble
scrabble

el dado
dice

la ficha
counter

el monopoly
monopoly

el backgammon | backgammon

los juegos de mesa | board games

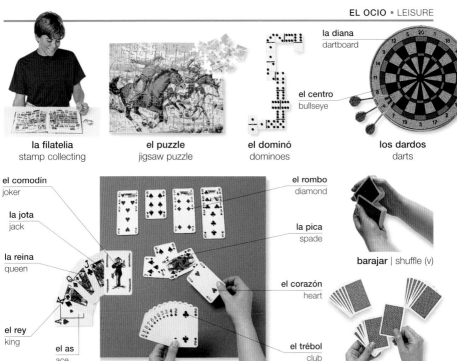

la diana
dartboard

el centro
bullseye

la filatelia
stamp collecting

el puzzle
jigsaw puzzle

el dominó
dominoes

los dardos
darts

el comodín
joker

el rombo
diamond

la jota
jack

la pica
spade

la reina
queen

barajar | shuffle (v)

el corazón
heart

el rey
king

el as
ace

el trébol
club

las cartas
cards

dar | deal (v)

---

vocabulario • vocabulary

el turno move	**ganar** win (v)	**el perdedor** loser	**el punto** point	**el bridge** bridge	**¿A quién le toca?** Whose turn is it?
jugar play (v)	**el ganador** winner	**la partida** game	**la puntuación** score	**la baraja** pack of cards	**Te toca a ti.** It's your move.
el jugador player	**perder** lose (v)	**la apuesta** bet	**el póquer** poker	**el palo** suit	**Tira los dados.** Roll the dice.

las manualidades 1 • arts and crafts 1

la pintora
artist

el cuadro
painting

el caballete
easel

el lienzo
canvas

el pincel
brush

la paleta
palette

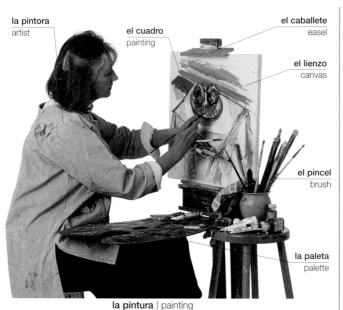

la pintura | painting

las pinturas • paints

las pinturas al óleo
oil paints

las acuarelas
watercolour paint

los pasteles
pastels

la pintura acrílica
acrylic paint

la témpera
poster paint

los colores • colours

rojo
red

azul blue	

azul
blue

amarillo
yellow

verde
green

naranja
orange

morado
purple

blanco
white

negro
black

gris
grey

rosa
pink

marrón
brown

azul añil
indigo

las otras manualidades • other crafts

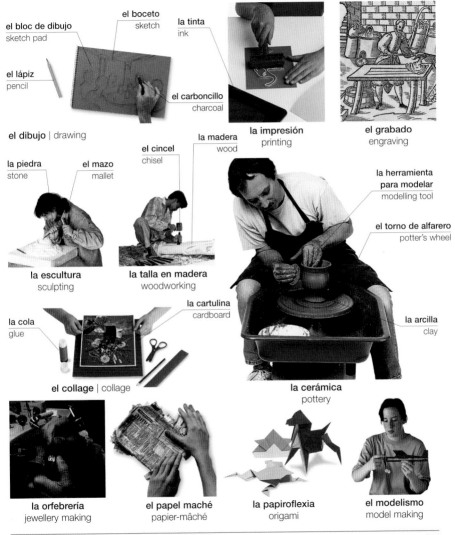

el bloc de dibujo
sketch pad

el lápiz
pencil

el boceto
sketch

la tinta
ink

el carboncillo
charcoal

el dibujo | drawing

la impresión
printing

el grabado
engraving

la piedra
stone

el mazo
mallet

el cincel
chisel

la madera
wood

la herramienta
para modelar
modelling tool

el torno de alfarero
potter's wheel

la escultura
sculpting

la talla en madera
woodworking

la arcilla
clay

la cola
glue

la cartulina
cardboard

el collage | collage

la cerámica
pottery

la orfebrería
jewellery making

el papel maché
papier-mâché

la papiroflexia
origami

el modelismo
model making

las manualidades 2 • arts and crafts 2

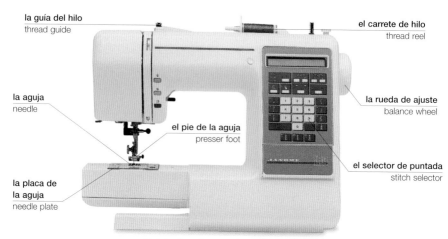

la guía del hilo
thread guide

el carrete de hilo
thread reel

la aguja
needle

el pie de la aguja
presser foot

la rueda de ajuste
balance wheel

la placa de
la aguja
needle plate

el selector de puntada
stitch selector

la máquina de coser | sewing machine

las tijeras
scissors

el patrón
pattern

el alfiletero
pincushion

la cinta métrica
tape measure

la tela
material

el alfiler
pin

el costurero | sewing basket

el hilo
thread

el ojo
eye

la bobina
bobbin

el corchete
hook

el dedal
thimble

el jaboncillo
tailor's chalk

el maniquí
tailor's dummy

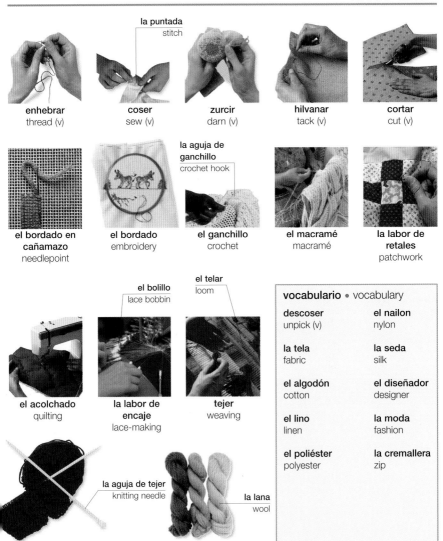

enhebrar
thread (v)

la puntada
stitch

coser
sew (v)

zurcir
darn (v)

hilvanar
tack (v)

cortar
cut (v)

el bordado en cañamazo
needlepoint

el bordado
embroidery

la aguja de ganchillo
crochet hook

el ganchillo
crochet

el macramé
macramé

la labor de retales
patchwork

el acolchado
quilting

el bolillo
lace bobbin

la labor de encaje
lace-making

el telar
loom

tejer
weaving

vocabulario • vocabulary

descoser
unpick (v)

la tela
fabric

el algodón
cotton

el lino
linen

el poliéster
polyester

el nailon
nylon

la seda
silk

el diseñador
designer

la moda
fashion

la cremallera
zip

la aguja de tejer
knitting needle

la labor de punto | knitting

la madeja | skein

la lana
wool

el medio ambiente
environment

el espacio • space

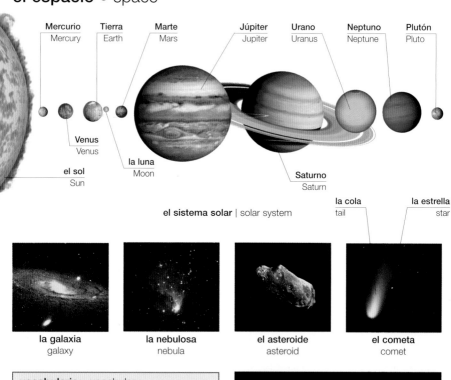

Mercurio Mercury	**Tierra** Earth	**Marte** Mars	**Júpiter** Jupiter	**Urano** Uranus	**Neptuno** Neptune	**Plutón** Pluto

Venus Venus

la luna Moon

el sol Sun

Saturno Saturn

el sistema solar | solar system

la cola tail

la estrella star

la galaxia
galaxy

la nebulosa
nebula

el asteroide
asteroid

el cometa
comet

vocabulario • vocabulary

el universo universe	**el planeta** planet	**la luna llena** full moon
la órbita orbit	**el meteorito** meteor	**la luna nueva** new moon
la gravedad gravity	**el agujero negro** black hole	**la media luna** crescent moon

el eclipse | eclipse

la exploración espacial • space exploration

el radar
radar

el propulsor
thruster

el trasbordador
espacial
space shuttle

la escotilla
crew hatch

el lanzacohetes
booster

el traje espacial
space suit

el astronauta | astronaut

el módulo lunar | lunar module

la rampa de
lanzamiento
launch pad

el lanzamiento
launch

el satélite
satellite

la estación espacial
space station

la astronomía • astronomy

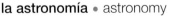

la constelación
constellation

los prismáticos
binoculars

el
telescopio
telescope

el trípode
tripod

la Tierra • Earth

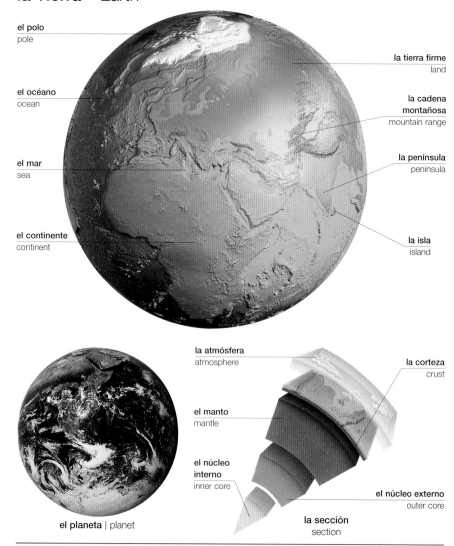

el polo
pole

el océano
ocean

el mar
sea

el continente
continent

la tierra firme
land

la cadena
montañosa
mountain range

la península
peninsula

la isla
island

la atmósfera
atmosphere

la corteza
crust

el manto
mantle

el núcleo
interno
inner core

el núcleo externo
outer core

la sección
section

el planeta | planet

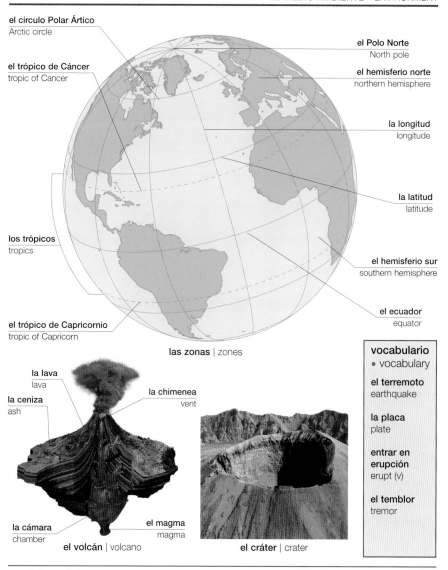

el círculo Polar Ártico
Arctic circle

el trópico de Cáncer
tropic of Cancer

los trópicos
tropics

el trópico de Capricornio
tropic of Capricorn

el Polo Norte
North pole

el hemisferio norte
northern hemisphere

la longitud
longitude

la latitud
latitude

el hemisferio sur
southern hemisphere

el ecuador
equator

las zonas | zones

la lava
lava

la ceniza
ash

la chimenea
vent

la cámara
chamber

el magma
magma

el volcán | volcano

el cráter | crater

vocabulario
• vocabulary

el terremoto
earthquake

la placa
plate

entrar en
erupción
erupt (v)

el temblor
tremor

el paisaje • landscape

la montaña
mountain

la ladera
slope

la orilla
bank

el río
river

los rápidos
rapids

las rocas
rocks

el glaciar
glacier

el valle | valley

la colina
hill

la meseta
plateau

el desfiladero
gorge

la cueva
cave

la llanura | plain

el desierto | desert

el bosque | forest

el bosque | wood

la selva tropical
rainforest

el pantano
swamp

el prado
meadow

la pradera
grassland

la cascada
waterfall

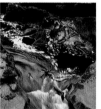
el arroyo
stream

el lago
lake

el géiser
geyser

la costa
coast

el acantilado
cliff

el arrecife de coral
coral reef

el estuario
estuary

el tiempo • weather

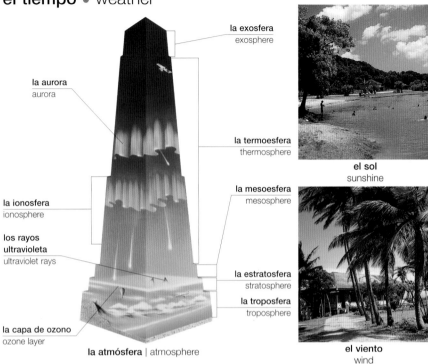

la exosfera
exosphere

la aurora
aurora

la termoesfera
thermosphere

la ionosfera
ionosphere

la mesoesfera
mesosphere

los rayos ultravioleta
ultraviolet rays

la estratosfera
stratosphere

la troposfera
troposphere

la capa de ozono
ozone layer

la atmósfera | atmosphere

el sol
sunshine

el viento
wind

vocabulario • vocabulary

el aguanieve sleet	el chubasco shower	caluroso hot	seco dry	ventoso windy	Tengo calor/frío. I'm hot/cold.
el granizo hail	soleado sunny	frío cold	lluvioso wet	el temporal gale	Está lloviendo. It's raining.
el trueno thunder	nublado cloudy	cálido warm	húmedo humid	la temperatura temperature	Estamos a … grados. It's … degrees.

el relámpago
lightning

la nube
cloud

la lluvia
rain

la tormenta
storm

la neblina
mist

la niebla
fog

el arcoiris
rainbow

el carámbano
icicle

la nieve
snow

la escarcha
frost

el hielo
ice

la helada
freeze

el huracán
hurricane

el tornado
tornado

el monzón
monsoon

la inundación
flood

las rocas • rocks

ígneo • igneous

el granito
granite

la obsidiana
obsidian

el basalto
basalt

la piedra pómez
pumice

sedimentario • sedimentary

la piedra arenisca
sandstone

la piedra caliza
limestone

la tiza
chalk

el pedernal
flint

el conglomerado
conglomerate

el carbón
coal

metamórfico •
metamorphic

la pizarra
slate

el esquisto
schist

el gneis
gneiss

el mármol
marble

las gemas • gems

el rubí
ruby

la aguamarina
aquamarine

la amatista
amethyst

el dia
mante
diamond

el jade
jade

el azabache
jet

la esmeralda
emerald

el ópalo
opal

el zafiro
sapphire

la piedra lunar
moonstone

el granate
garnet

el topacio
topaz

la turmalina
tourmaline

los minerales • minerals

el cuarzo
quartz

la mica
mica

el azufre
sulphur

el hematites
hematite

la calcita
calcite

la malaquita
malachite

la turquesa
turquoise

el ónice
onyx

el ágata
agate

el grafito
graphite

los metales • metals

el oro
gold

la plata
silver

el platino
platinum

el níquel
nickel

el hierro
iron

el cobre
copper

el estaño
tin

el aluminio
aluminium

el mercurio
mercury

el zinc
zinc

los animales 1 • animals 1
los mamíferos • mammals

el conejo
rabbit

el hámster
hamster

los bigotes
whiskers

el ratón
mouse

la cola
tail

la rata
rat

el erizo
hedgehog

la ardilla
squirrel

el murciélago
bat

el mapache
raccoon

el zorro
fox

el lobo
wolf

el cachorro
puppy

el gatito
kitten

la cría
pup

el perro
dog

el gato
cat

la nutria
otter

la foca
seal

el león marino
sea lion

la aleta
flipper

la morsa
walrus

el orificio nasal
blowhole

la ballena
whale

el delfín
dolphin

el asta
antler

la crin
mane

la giba
hump

el ciervo
deer

la pezuña
hoof

la cebra
zebra

la jirafa
giraffe

el camello
camel

la trompa
trunk

el colmillo
tusk

el cuerno
horn

el hipopótamo
hippopotamus

el elefante
elephant

el rinoceronte
rhinoceros

el tigre
tiger

la melena
mane

el león
lion

el mono
monkey

el gorila
gorilla

el koala
koala

la bolsa
pouch

el oso panda
panda

la zarpa
claw

el canguro
kangaroo

el oso
bear

el oso polar
polar bear

los animales 2 • animals 2
las aves • birds

la cola
tail

el canario
canary

el gorrión
sparrow

el colibrí
hummingbird

la golondrina
swallow

el cuervo
crow

la paloma
pigeon

el pájaro carpintero
woodpecker

el halcón
falcon

el búho
owl

la gaviota
gull

el águila
eagle

el pelícano
pelican

el flamenco
flamingo

la cigüeña
stork

la grulla
crane

el pingüino
penguin

el avestruz
ostrich

la oca | goose

el cisne
swan

el pavo real
peacock

el faisán
pheasant

el pavo
turkey

el pico
bill

la pluma
feather

el ala
wing

la cacatúa
cockatoo

la garra
claw

el loro
parrot

los reptiles • reptiles

las escamas
scales

el caimán
alligator

el lagarto
lizard

la iguana
iguana

el caparazón
shell

el galápago
turtle

la tortuga
tortoise

la serpiente
snake

el hocico
snout

el cocodrilo
crocodile

los animales 3 • animals 3
los anfibios • amphibians

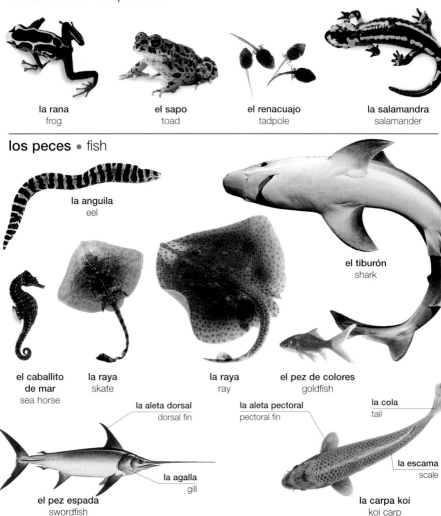

la rana	**el sapo**	**el renacuajo**	**la salamandra**
frog	toad	tadpole	salamander

los peces • fish

la anguila
eel

el tiburón
shark

el caballito de mar
sea horse

la raya
skate

la raya
ray

el pez de colores
goldfish

la aleta dorsal
dorsal fin

la aleta pectoral
pectoral fin

la cola
tail

la agalla
gill

la escama
scale

el pez espada
swordfish

la carpa koi
koi carp

los invertebrados • invertebrates

la hormiga
ant

la termita
termite

la abeja
bee

la avispa
wasp

el escarabajo
beetle

la cucaracha
cockroach

la polilla
moth

la mariposa
butterfly

la antena
antenna

el capullo
cocoon

la oruga
caterpillar

el grillo
cricket

el saltamontes
grasshopper

la mantis religiosa
praying mantis

el aquijón
sting

el escorpión
scorpion

el ciempiés
centipede

la libélula
dragonfly

la mosca
fly

el mosquito
mosquito

la mariquita
ladybird

la araña
spider

la babosa
slug

el caracol
snail

el gusano
worm

la estrella de mar
starfish

el mejillón
mussel

el cangrejo
crab

la langosta
lobster

el pulpo
octopus

el calamar
squid

la medusa
jellyfish

las plantas • plants

el árbol • tree

la rama
branch

la hoja
leaf

la ramita
twig

la corteza
bark

la raíz
root

el tronco
trunk

el roble
oak

el sauce
willow

el álamo
poplar

el eucalipto
eucalyptus

el alerce
larch

la haya
beech

el abedul
birch

el pino
pine

el cedro
cedar

el arce
maple

el olmo
elm

el tilo
lime

el acebo
holly

la baya
berry

la palmera
palm

la planta de flor • flowering plant

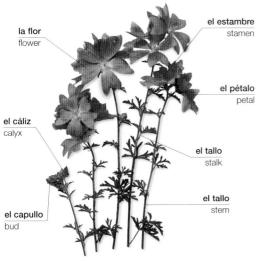

la flor
flower

el cáliz
calyx

el capullo
bud

el estambre
stamen

el pétalo
petal

el tallo
stalk

el tallo
stem

el ranúnculo
buttercup

la margarita
daisy

el cardo
thistle

el diente de león
dandelion

el brezo
heather

la amapola
poppy

la dedalera
foxglove

la madreselva
honeysuckle

el girasol
sunflower

el trébol
clover

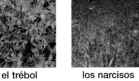

los narcisos silvestres
bluebells

la prímula
primrose

el lupino
lupins

la ortiga
nettle

la ciudad • town

la calle
street

el bordillo
kerb

la esquina
street corner

la tienda
shop

el cruce
intersection

la calle de
sentido único
one-way
system

la acera
pavement

el edificio
de oficinas
office block

el edificio
de pisos
apartment
block

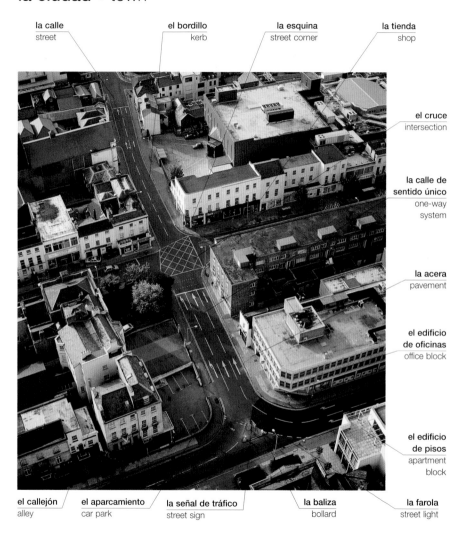

el callejón
alley

el aparcamiento
car park

la señal de tráfico
street sign

la baliza
bollard

la farola
street light

los edificios • buildings

el ayuntamiento
town hall

la biblioteca
library

el cine
cinema

el teatro
theatre

la universidad
university

el rascacielos
skyscraper

las zonas • areas

la zona industrial
industrial estate

la ciudad
city

la periferia
suburb

el pueblo
village

el colegio
school

---

vocabulario • vocabulary

la zona peatonal pedestrian zone	**la calle lateral** side street	**la boca de alcantarilla** manhole	**la alcantarilla** gutter	**la iglesia** church
la avenida avenue	**la plaza** square	**la parada de autobús** bus stop	**la fábrica** factory	**el sumidero** drain

la arquitectura • architecture

los edificios y las estructuras • buildings and structures

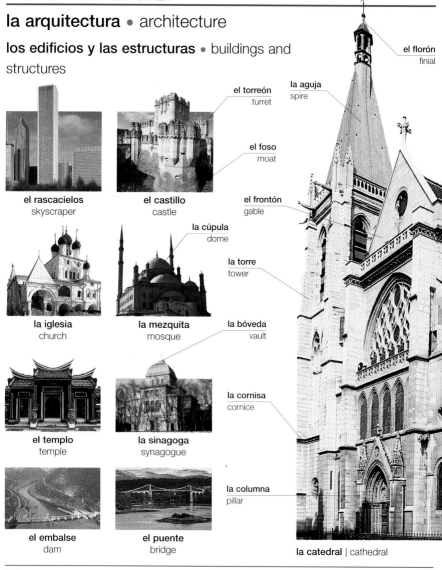

el rascacielos
skyscraper

el torreón
turret

el foso
moat

el castillo
castle

la iglesia
church

la cúpula
dome

la mezquita
mosque

el templo
temple

la sinagoga
synagogue

el embalse
dam

el puente
bridge

el florón
finial

la aguja
spire

el frontón
gable

la torre
tower

la bóveda
vault

la cornisa
cornice

la columna
pillar

la catedral | cathedral

los estilos • styles

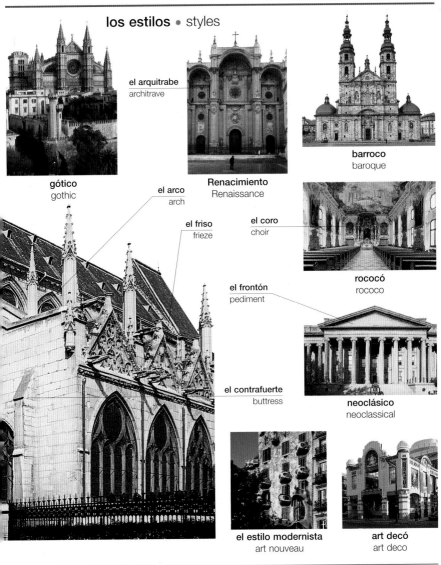

gótico
gothic

el arquitrabe
architrave

Renacimiento
Renaissance

barroco
baroque

el arco
arch

el friso
frieze

el coro
choir

rococó
rococo

el frontón
pediment

el contrafuerte
buttress

neoclásico
neoclassical

el estilo modernista
art nouveau

art decó
art deco

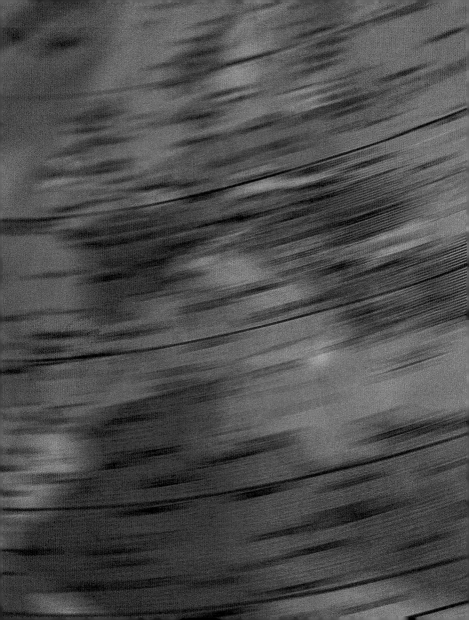

los datos
reference

el tiempo • time

el minutero
minute hand

la aguja de la hora
hour hand

el reloj
clock

vocabulario • vocabulary

el segundo second	**ahora** now	**un cuarto de hora** a quarter of an hour
el minuto minute	**más tarde** later	**veinte minutos** twenty minutes
la hora hour	**media hora** half an hour	**cuarenta minutos** forty minutes

¿Qué hora es?
What time is it?

Son las tres en punto.
It's three o'clock.

la una y cinco
five past one

la una y diez
ten past one

la una y cuarto
quarter past one

la una y veinte
twenty past one

la trotteuse
second hand

la una y veinticinco
twenty five past one

la una y media
one thirty

las dos menos veinticinco
twenty five to two

las dos menos veinte
twenty to two

las dos menos cuarto
quarter to two

las dos menos diez
ten to two

las dos menos cinco
five to two

las dos en punto
two o'clock

la noche y el día • night and day

la medianoche
midnight

el amanecer
sunrise

el alba
dawn

la mañana
morning

la puesta de sol
sunset

el mediodía
midday

el anochecer
dusk

la noche
evening

la tarde
afternoon

---

vocabulario • vocabulary

temprano early	**Llegas temprano.** You're early.	**Por favor, sé puntual.** Please be on time.	**¿A qué hora termina?** What time does it finish?
puntual on time	**Llegas tarde.** You're late.	**Hasta luego.** I'll see you later.	**¿Cuánto dura?** How long will it last?
tarde late	**Llegaré dentro de poco.** I'll be there soon.	**¿A qué hora comienza?** What time does it start?	**Se está haciendo tarde.** It's getting late.

el almanaque • calendar

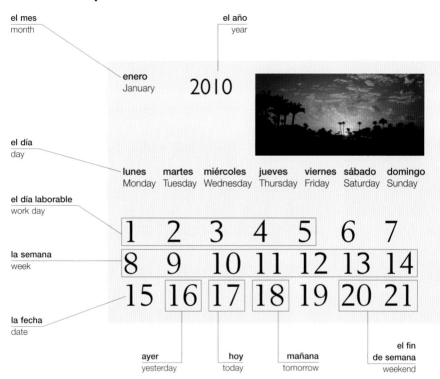

el mes
month

el año
year

enero
January

2010

el día
day

lunes	**martes**	**miércoles**	**jueves**	**viernes**	**sábado**	**domingo**
Monday	Tuesday	Wednesday	Thursday	Friday	Saturday	Sunday

el día laborable
work day

la semana
week

1	2	3	4	5	6	7
8	9	10	11	12	13	14
15	16	17	18	19	20	21

la fecha
date

ayer
yesterday

hoy
today

mañana
tomorrow

el fin de semana
weekend

---

vocabulario • vocabulary

enero	**marzo**	**mayo**	**julio**	**septiembre**	**noviembre**
January	March	May	July	September	November
febrero	**abril**	**junio**	**agosto**	**octubre**	**diciembre**
February	April	June	August	October	December

---

los años • years

1900   **mil novecientos** • nineteen hundred

1901   **mil novecientos uno** • nineteen hundred and one

1910   **mil novecientos diez** • nineteen ten

2000   **dos mil** • two thousand

2001   **dos mil uno** • two thousand and one

las estaciones • seasons

la primavera
spring

el verano
summer

el otoño
autumn

el invierno
winter

---

vocabulario • vocabulary

el siglo
century

la década
decade

el milenio
millennium

quince días
fortnight

esta semana
this week

la semana pasada
last week

la semana que viene
next week

antes de ayer
the day before yesterday

pasado mañana
the day after tomorrow

semanalmente
weekly

mensual
monthly

anual
annual

¿Qué día es hoy?
What's the date today?

Es el siete de febrero del dos mil dos.
It's February seventh, two thousand and two.

los números • numbers

0	cero • zero		20	veinte • twenty
1	uno • one		21	veintiuno • twenty-one
2	dos • two		22	veintidós • twenty-two
3	tres • three		30	treinta • thirty
4	cuatro • four		40	cuarenta • forty
5	cinco • five		50	cincuenta • fifty
6	seis • six		60	sesenta • sixty
7	siete • seven		70	setenta • seventy
8	ocho • eight		80	ochenta • eighty
9	nueve • nine		90	noventa • ninety
10	diez • ten		100	cien • one hundred
11	once • eleven		110	ciento diez • one hundred and ten
12	doce • twelve		200	doscientos • two hundred
13	trece • thirteen		300	trescientos • three hundred
14	catorce • fourteen		400	cuatrocientos • four hundred
15	quince • fifteen		500	quinientos • five hundred
16	dieciséis • sixteen		600	seiscientos • six hundred
17	diecisiete • seventeen		700	setecientos • seven hundred
18	dieciocho • eighteen		800	ochocientos • eight hundred
19	diecinueve • nineteen		900	novecientos • nine hundred

español • english

1,000 — **mil** • one thousand

10,000 — **diez mil** • ten thousand

20,000 — **veinte mil** • twenty thousand

50,000 — **cincuenta mil** • fifty thousand

55,500 — **cincuenta y cinco mil quinientos** • fifty-five thousand five hundred

100,000 — **cien mil** • one hundred thousand

1,000,000 — **un millón** • one million

1,000,000,000 — **mil millones** • one billion

primero
first

segundo
second

tercero
third

cuarto • fourth

quinto • fifth

sexto • sixth

séptimo • seventh

octavo • eighth

noveno • ninth

décimo • tenth

undécimo • eleventh

duodécimo • twelfth

decimotercero • thirteenth

decimocuarto • fourteenth

decimoquinto • fifteenth

decimosexto
• sixteenth

decimoséptimo
• seventeenth

décimo octavo
• eighteenth

décimo noveno
• nineteenth

vigésimo
• twentieth

vigésimo primero
• twenty-first

vigésimo segundo
• twenty-second

vigésimo tercero
• twenty-third

trigésimo • thirtieth

cuadragésimo
• fortieth

quincuagésimo
• fiftieth

sexagésimo • sixtieth

septuagésimo
• seventieth

octogésimo
• eightieth

nonagésimo
• ninetieth

centésimo
• hundredth

los pesos y las medidas • weights and measures

el área • area

el pie cuadrado
square foot

el metro cuadrado
square metre

la distancia • distance

el kilómetro
kilometre

la milla
mile

la bandeja
pan

el kilogramo
kilogram

el gramo
gram

la libra
pound

la onza
ounce

la balanza | scales

vocabulario • vocabulary

la yarda yard	**la tonelada** tonne	**medir** measure (v)
el metro metre	**el miligramo** milligram	**pesar** weigh (v)

la longitud • length

el pie
foot

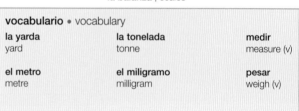

el milímetro
millimetre

el centímetro
centimetre

la pulgada
inch

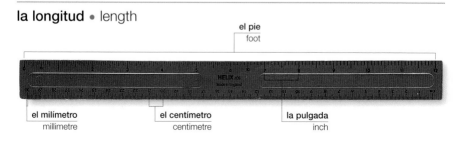

la capacidad • capacity

el medio litro
half-litre

la pinta
pint

el volumen
volume

el mililitro
mililitre

la jarra graduada
measuring jug

la medida de capacidad
liquid measure

el recipiente • container

la bolsa
bag

el tetrabrik
carton

el paquete
packet

la botella
bottle

la tarrina | tub

el tarro | jar

la lata
can

la lata | tin

el pulverizador
liquid dispenser

la pastilla
bar

el tubo
tube

el rollo
roll

el paquete
pack

el spray
spray can

el mapamundi • world map

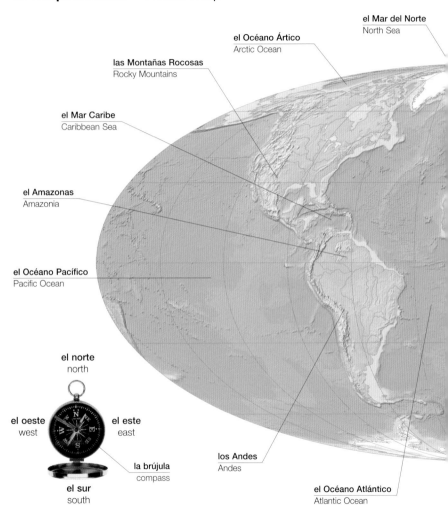

el Mar del Norte
North Sea

el Océano Ártico
Arctic Ocean

las Montañas Rocosas
Rocky Mountains

el Mar Caribe
Caribbean Sea

el Amazonas
Amazonia

el Océano Pacífico
Pacific Ocean

el norte
north

el oeste
west

el este
east

la brújula
compass

los Andes
Andes

el Océano Atlántico
Atlantic Ocean

el sur
south

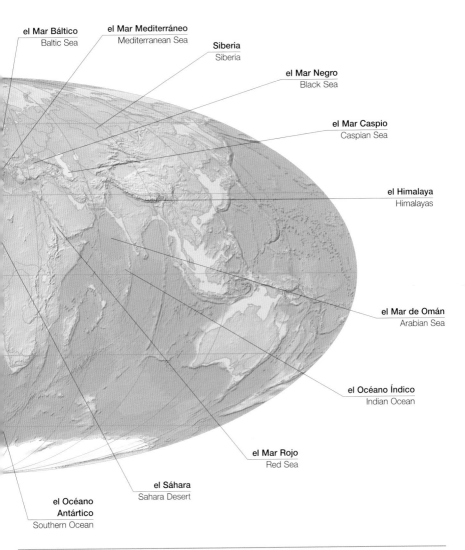

el Mar Báltico
Baltic Sea

el Mar Mediterráneo
Mediterranean Sea

Siberia
Siberia

el Mar Negro
Black Sea

el Mar Caspio
Caspian Sea

el Himalaya
Himalayas

el Mar de Omán
Arabian Sea

el Océano Índico
Indian Ocean

el Mar Rojo
Red Sea

el Sáhara
Sahara Desert

el Océano
Antártico
Southern Ocean

América del Norte y Central • North and Central America

Hawaii
Hawaii

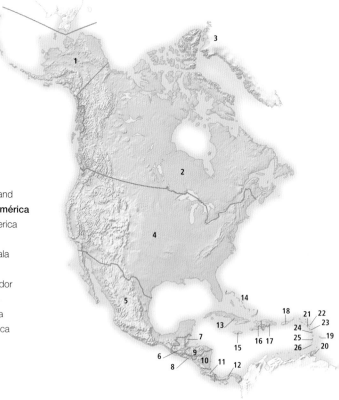

1 **Alaska** • Alaska

2 **Canadá** • Canada

3 **Groenlandia** • Greenland

4 **Estados Unidos de América**
   • United States of America

5 **México** • Mexico

6 **Guatemala** • Guatemala

7 **Belice** • Belize

8 **El Salvador** • El Salvador

9 **Honduras** • Honduras

10 **Nicaragua** • Nicaragua

11 **Costa Rica** • Costa Rica

12 **Panamá** • Panama

13 **Cuba** • Cuba

14 **Bahamas** • Bahamas

15 **Jamaica** • Jamaica

16 **Haití** • Haiti

17 **República Dominicana**
   • Dominican Republic

18 **Puerto Rico** • Puerto Rico

19 **Barbados** • Barbados

20 **Trinidad y Tobago** • Trinidad and Tobago

21 **Saint Kitts y Nevis** • St. Kitts and Nevis

22 **Antigua y Barbuda** • Antigua and Barbuda

23 **Dominica** • Dominica

24 **Santa Lucía** • St Lucia

25 **San Vicente y las Granadinas**
   • St Vincent and The Grenadines

26 **Granada** • Grenada

América del Sur • South America

1 **Venezuela** • Venezuela

2 **Colombia** • Colombia

3 **Ecuador** • Ecuador

4 **Perú** • Peru

5 **las Islas Galápagos**
 • Galapagos Islands

6 **Guyana** • Guyana

7 **Suriname** • Suriname

8 **la Guayana Francesa**
 • French Guiana

9 **Brasil** • Brazil

10 **Bolivia** • Bolivia

11 **Chile** • Chile

12 **Argentina** • Argentina

13 **Paraguay** • Paraguay

14 **Uruguay** • Uruguay

15 **las Malvinas** • Falkland Islands

vocabulario • vocabulary

el continente continent	**el principado** principality	**la provincia** province
el país country	**el territorio** territory	**el distrito** district
la nación nation	**la colonia** colony	**la región** region
el estado state	**la zona** zone	**la capital** capital

Europa • Europe

1 **Irlanda** • Ireland
2 **Reino Unido** • United Kingdom
3 **Portugal** • Portugal
4 **España** • Spain
5 **las Islas Baleares**
   • Balearic Islands
6 **Andorra** • Andorra
7 **Francia** • France
8 **Bélgica** • Belgium
9 **los Países Bajos**
   • Netherlands
10 **Luxemburgo** • Luxembourg
11 **Alemania** • Germany
12 **Dinamarca** • Denmark
13 **Noruega** • Norway
14 **Suecia** • Sweden
15 **Finlandia** • Finland
16 **Estonia** • Estonia
17 **Letonia** • Latvia
18 **Lituania** • Lithuania
19 **Kaliningrado** • Kaliningrad
20 **Polonia** • Poland
21 **República Checa**
   • Czech Republic
22 **Austria** • Austria
23 **Liechtenstein**
   • Liechtenstein
24 **Suiza**
   • Switzerland
25 **Italia** • Italy
26 **Mónaco**
   • Monaco
27 **Córcega**
   • Corsica
28 **Cerdeña**
   • Sardinia
29 **San Marino** • San Marino

30 **la Ciudad del Vaticano**
   • Vatican City
31 **Sicilia** • Sicily
32 **Malta** • Malta
33 **Eslovenia** • Slovenia
34 **Croacia** • Croatia
35 **Hungría** • Hungary
36 **Eslovaquia** • Slovakia
37 **Ucrania** • Ukraine
38 **Belarús** • Belarus
39 **Moldavia** • Moldova

40 **Rumanía** • Romania
41 **Serbia** • Serbia
42 **Bosnia y Herzegovina**
   • Bosnia and Herzegovina
43 **Albania** • Albania
44 **Macedonia** • Macedonia
45 **Bulgaria** • Bulgaria
46 **Grecia** • Greece
47 **Kosovo** • Kosovo
48 **Montenegro** • Montenegro
49 **Islandia** • Iceland

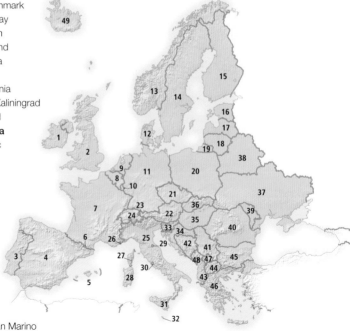

África • Africa

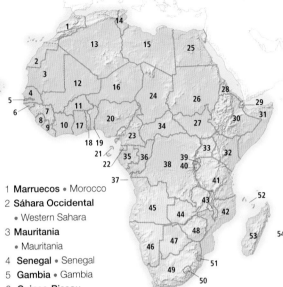

1 **Marruecos** • Morocco
2 **Sáhara Occidental**
   • Western Sahara
3 **Mauritania**
   • Mauritania
4 **Senegal** • Senegal
5 **Gambia** • Gambia
6 **Guinea-Bissau**
   • Guinea-Bissau
7 **Guinea** • Guinea
8 **Sierra Leona**
   • Sierra Leone
9 **Liberia** • Liberia
10 **Costa de Marfil**
    • Ivory Coast
11 **Burquina Faso**
    • Burkina Faso
12 **Malí** • Mali
13 **Argelia** • Algeria
14 **Túnez** • Tunisia
15 **Libia** • Libya
16 **Níger** • Niger
17 **Ghana** • Ghana
18 **Togo** • Togo

19 **Benin** • Benin
20 **Nigeria** • Nigeria
21 **Santo Tomé y Príncipe**
    • São Tomé and Principe
22 **Guinea Ecuatorial**
    • Equatorial Guinea
23 **Camerún** • Cameroon
24 **Chad** • Chad
25 **Egipto** • Egypt
26 **Sudán** • Sudan
27 **Sudán del Sur** • South Sudan
28 **Eritrea** • Eritrea
29 **Djibouti** • Djibouti
30 **Etiopía** • Ethiopia
31 **Somalia** • Somalia

32 **Kenya** • Kenya
33 **Uganda** • Uganda
34 **República Centroafricana**
    • Central African Republic
35 **Gabón** • Gabon
36 **Congo** • Congo
37 **Cabinda** • Cabinda
38 **República Democrática del**
    Congo • Democratic
    Republic of the Congo
39 **Rwanda** • Rwanda
40 **Burundi** • Burundi
41 **Tanzania** • Tanzania
42 **Mozambique** • Mozambique
43 **Malawi** • Malawi
44 **Zambia** • Zambia
45 **Angola** • Angola
46 **Namibia** • Namibia
47 **Botswana** • Botswana
48 **Zimbabwe** • Zimbabwe
49 **Sudáfrica** • South Africa
50 **Lesotho** • Lesotho
51 **Swazilandia** • Swaziland
52 **Comoros** • Comoros
53 **Madagascar** • Madagascar
54 **Mauricio** • Mauritius

Asia • Asia

1 **la Turchia** • Turkey
2 **Cipro** • Cyprus
3 **Federación Rusa**
   • Russian Federation
4 **Georgia** • Georgia
5 **Armenia** • Armenia
6 **Azerbaiyán** • Azerbaijan
7 **Irán** • Iran
8 **Iraq** • Iraq
9 **Siria** • Syria
10 **Líbano** • Lebanon
11 **Israel** • Israel
12 **Jordania** • Jordan
13 **Arabia Saudita**
   • Saudi Arabia
14 **Kuwait** • Kuwait
15 **Bahrein** • Bahrain
16 **Qatar** • Qatar
17 **Emiratos Árabes Unidos**
   • United Arab Emirates
18 **Omán** • Oman
19 **Yemen** • Yemen
20 **Kazajstán** • Kazakhstan
21 **Uzbekistán** • Uzbekistan
22 **Turkmenistán** • Turkmenistan
23 **Afganistán** • Afghanistan
24 **Tayikistán** • Tajikistan
25 **Kirguistán** • Kyrgyzstan
26 **Pakistán** • Pakistan
27 **India** • India
28 **Maldivas** • Maldives
29 **Sri Lanka** • Sri Lanka
30 **China** • China
31 **Mongolia** • Mongolia
32 **Corea del Norte** • North Korea
33 **Corea del Sur** • South Korea
34 **Japón** • Japan

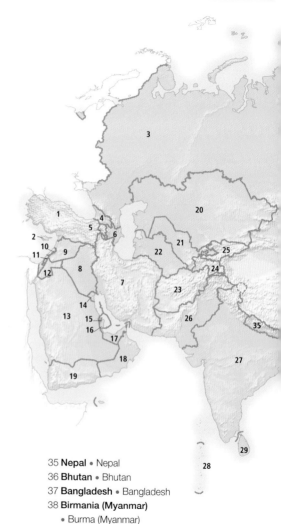

35 **Nepal** • Nepal
36 **Bhutan** • Bhutan
37 **Bangladesh** • Bangladesh
38 **Birmania (Myanmar)**
   • Burma (Myanmar)
39 **Tailandia** • Thailand
40 **Laos** • Laos

español • english

Australasia • Australasia

1 **Australia** • Australia
2 **Tasmania** • Tasmania
3 **Nueva Zelandia** • New Zealand

41 **Viet Nam** • Vietnam
42 **Camboya** • Cambodia
43 **Malasia** • Malaysia
44 **Singapur** • Singapore
45 **Indonesia** • Indonesia
46 **Brunei** • Brunei
47 **Filipinas** • Philippines
48 **Timor Oriental** • East Timor
49 **Papua Nueva Guinea** • Papua New Guinea
50 **Islas Salomón** • Solomon Islands
51 **Vanuatu** • Vanuatu
52 **Fiji** • Fiji

partículas y antónimos • particles and antonyms

a, hacia to	**de, desde** from	**para** for	**hacia** towards
encima de over	**debajo de** under	**por** along	**al otro lado de** across
delante de in front of	**detrás de** behind	**con** with	**sin** without
sobre onto	**dentro de** into	**antes** before	**después** after
en in	**fuera** out	**antes de** by	**hasta** until
sobre above	**bajo** below	**temprano** early	**tarde** late
dentro inside	**fuera** outside	**ahora** now	**más tarde** later
arriba up	**abajo** down	**siempre** always	**nunca** never
en at	**más allá de** beyond	**a menudo** often	**rara vez** rarely
a través de through	**alrededor de** around	**ayer** yesterday	**mañana** tomorrow
encima de on top of	**al lado de** beside	**primer** first	**último** last
entre between	**en frente de** opposite	**cada** every	**algunos** some
cerca near	**lejos** far	**unos** about	**exactamente** exactly
aquí here	**allí** there	**un poco** a little	**mucho** a lot

español	english		español	english
grande large	**pequeño** small		**caliente** hot	**frío** cold
ancho wide	**estrecho** narrow		**abierto** open	**cerrado** closed
alto tall	**bajo** short		**lleno** full	**vacío** empty
alto high	**bajo** low		**nuevo** new	**viejo** old
grueso thick	**delgado** thin		**claro** light	**oscuro** dark
ligero light	**pesado** heavy		**fácil** easy	**difícil** difficult
duro hard	**blando** soft		**libre** free	**ocupado** occupied
húmedo wet	**seco** dry		**fuerte** strong	**débil** weak
bueno good	**malo** bad		**gordo** fat	**delgado** thin
rápido fast	**lento** slow		**joven** young	**viejo** old
correcto correct	**incorrecto** wrong		**mejor** better	**peor** worse
limpio clean	**sucio** dirty		**negro** black	**blanco** white
bonito beautiful	**feo** ugly		**interesante** interesting	**aburrido** boring
caro expensive	**barato** cheap		**enfermo** sick	**bien** well
silencioso quiet	**ruidoso** noisy		**el principio** beginning	**el final** end

frases útiles • useful phrases

frases esenciales
• essential phrases

Sí
Yes

No
No

Quizá
Maybe

Por favor
Please

Gracias
Thank you

De nada
You're welcome

Perdone
Excuse me

Lo siento
I'm sorry

No
Don't

Vale
OK

Así vale
That's fine

Está bien
That's correct

Está mal
That's wrong

saludos • greetings

Hola
Hello

Adiós
Goodbye

Buenos días
Good morning

Buenas tardes
Good afternoon

Buenas tardes
Good evening

Buenas noches
Good night

¿Cómo está?
How are you?

Me llamo…
My name is…

¿Cómo se llama?
What is your name?

¿Cómo se llama?
What is his/her name?

Le presento a…
May I introduce…

Este es…
This is…

Encantado de conocerle
Pleased to meet you

Hasta luego
See you later

letreros • signs

Información
Tourist information

Entrada
Entrance

Salida
Exit

Salida de emergencia
Emergency exit

Empuje
Push

Peligro
Danger

Prohibido fumar
No smoking

Fuera de servicio
Out of order

Horario de apertura
Opening times

Entrada libre
Free admission

Llame antes de entrar
Knock before entering

Rebajado
Reduced

Saldos
Sale

Prohibido pisar el césped
Keep off the grass

ayuda • help

¿Me puede ayudar?
Can you help me?

No entiendo
I don't understand

No lo sé
I don't know

¿Habla inglés, francés…?
Do you speak English, French…?

Hablo inglés, español…
I speak English, Spanish…

Hable más despacio, por favor
Please speak more slowly

¿Me lo puede escribir?
Please write it down for me

He perdido…
I have lost…

322

indicaciones
• directions

Me he perdido
I am lost

¿Dónde está el/la...?
Where is the...?

¿Dónde está el/la... más cercano/a?
Where is the nearest...?

¿Dónde están los servicios?
Where are the toilets?

¿Cómo voy a...?
How do I get to...?

A la derecha
To the right

A la izquierda
To the left

Todo recto
Straight ahead

¿A qué distancia está...?
How far is...?

las señales de tráfico
• road signs

Todas las direcciones
All directions

Precaución
Caution

Prohibida la entrada
No entry

Disminuir velocidad
Slow down

Desvío
Diversion

Circular por la derecha
Keep to the right

Autopista
Motorway

Prohibido aparcar
No parking

Callejón sin salida
No through road

Sentido único
One-way

Ceda el paso
Give way

Carretera cortada
Road closed

Obras
Roadworks

Curva peligrosa
Dangerous bend

alojamiento
• accommodation

Tengo una reserva
I have a reservation

¿A qué hora es el desayuno?
What time is breakfast?

El número de mi habitación es el ...
My room number is ...

Voleré a las ...
I'll be back at ... o'clock

¿Dónde está el comedor?
Where is the dining room?

Me marcho mañana
I'm leaving tomorrow

comida y bebida
• eating and drinking

¡Salud!
Cheers!

Está buenísimo/malísimo
It's delicious/awful

Yo no bebo/fumo
I don't drink/smoke

Yo no como carne
I don't eat meat

Ya no más, gracias
No more for me, thank you

¿Puedo repetir?
May I have some more?

¿Me trae la cuenta?
May we have the bill?

¿Me da un recibo?
Can I have a receipt?

Zona de no fumadores
No-smoking area

la salud
• health

No me encuentro bien
I don't feel well

Tengo náuseas
I feel sick

¿Cuál es el número del médico más cercano?
What is the telephone number of the nearest doctor?

Me duele aquí
It hurts here

Tengo fiebre
I have a temperature

Estoy embarazada de ... meses
I'm ... months pregnant

Necesito una receta para ...
I need a prescription for ...

Normalmente tomo ...
I normally take ...

Soy alérgico a ...
I'm allergic to ...

¿Estará bien?
Will he/she be all right?

índice español • Spanish index

español

A

español

español

ÍNDICE ESPAÑOL • SPANISH INDEX

español

español • english

español

español

español

español

español

español

español • english

español

español

español

índice inglés • English index

english

english

english

english

english

english

english

español • english

english

english

english

english

english

agradecimientos • acknowledgments

DORLING KINDERSLEY would like to thank Tracey Miles and Christine Lacey for design assistance, Georgina Garner for editorial and administrative help, Sonia Gavira, Polly Boyd, and Cathy Meeus for editorial help, and Claire Bowers for compiling the DK picture credits.

The publisher would like to thank the following for their kind permission to reproduce their photographs:

Abbreviations key: a-above; b-below/bottom; c-centre; f-far; l-left; r-right; t-top

123RF.com: Andriy Popov 34tl; Daniel Ernst 179tc; Hongqi Zhang 24cla. 175cr; Ingvar Bjork 60c; Kobby Dagan 259c; leonardo255 269c; Liubov Vadimovna (Luba) Nel 39cla; Ljupco Smokovski 75crb; Oleksandr Marynchenko 60bl; Olga Popova 33c; oneblink 49bc; Racorn 162tl; Robert Churchill 94c; Roman Gorielov 33bc; Ruslan Kudrin 35bc, 35br; Subbotina 39cra; Sutichak Yachaingkham 39tc; Tarzhanova 37tc; Vitaly Valua 39tl; Wavebreak Media Ltd 188bl; Wilawan Khasawong 75cb; **Action Plus:** 224bc; **Alamy Images:** 154t; A.T. Willett 287bcl; Alex Segre 105ca, 105cb, 195cl; Ambrophoto 24cra; Blend Images 168cr; Cultura RM 33r; Doug Houghton 107fbr; Ekkapon Sriharun 172bl; Hugh Threlfall 35tl; 176tr; Ian Allenden 48br; Ian Dagnall (iPod is a trademark of Apple Inc., registered in the U.S. and other countries) 268tc, 270t; Ievgen Chepil 250bc; imagebroker 199tl, 249c; keith morris 178c; Martyn Evans 210b; MBI 175tl; Michael Burrell 213cra; Michael Foyle 184bl; Oleksiy Maksymenko 105tc; Paul Weston 168br; Prisma Bildagentur AG 246b; Radharc Images 197tr; RBtravel 112tl; Ruslan Kudrin 176tl; Sasa Huzjak 258t; Sergey Kravchenko 37ca; Sergio Azenha 270bc; Stanca Sanda (iPad is a trademark of Apple Inc., registered in the U.S. and other countries) 176bc; Stock Connection 287bcr; tarczas 35cr; vitaly suprun 176cl; Wavebreak Media ltd 39cl, 174b, 175r; **Allsport/Getty Images:** 238cl; **Alvey and Towers:** 209 acr, 215bcl, 215bcr, 241cr; **Peter Anderson:** 188cbr, 271br. **Anthony Blake Photo Library:** Charlie Stebbings 114cl; John Sims 114tcl; **Andyalte:** 98tl; **apple mac computers:** 268tcr; **Arcaid:** John Edward Linden 301bl; Martine Hamilton Knight, Architects: Chapman Taylor Partners, 213cl; Richard Bryant 301br; **Argos:** 41tcl, 66cbl, 66cl, 66br, 66bcl, 69cl, 70bcl, 71t, 77tl, 269tc, 270tl; **Axiom:** Eitan Simanor 105bcr; Ian Cumming 104; Vicki Couchman 148cr; **Beken Of Cowes Ltd:** 215cbr; **Bosch:** 76cr, 76tc, 76tcl; **Camera Press:** 38tr, 256t, 257cr; Barry J. Holmes 148tr; Jane Hanger 159cr; Mary Germanou 259bc; **Corbis:** 78b; Anna Clopet 247tr; Ariel Skelley / Blend Images 52l; Bettmann 181tl, 181tr; Blue Jean Images 48bl; Bo Zauders 156t; Bob Rowan 152bl; Bob Winsett 247cbl; Brian Bailey 247br; Carl and Ann Purcell 162l; Chris Rainer 247ctl; Craig Aurness 215bl; David H.Wells 249cbr; Dennis Marsico

274bl; Dimitri Lundt 236bc; Duomo 211tl; Gail Mooney 277ctcr; George Lepp 248c; Gerald Nowak 239b; Gunter Marx 248cr; Jack Hollingsworth 231bl; Jacqui Hurst 277cbr; James L. Amos 247bl, 191ctr, 220bcr; Jan Butchofsky 277cbc; Johnathan Blair 243cr; Jose F. Poblete 191br; Jose Luis Pelaez.Inc 153tc; Karl Weatherly 220bl, 247tcr; Kelly Mooney Photography 259tl; Kevin Fleming 249bc; Kevin R. Morris 105tr, 243tl, 243tc; Kim Sayer 249tcr; Lynn Goldsmith 258t; Macduff Everton 231bcl; Mark Gibson 249bl; Mark L. Stephenson 249tcl; Michael Pole 115tr; Michael S. Yamashita 247ctcl; Mike King 247cbl; Neil Rabinowitz 214br; Pablo Corral 115bc; Paul A. Sounders 169br, 249ctcl; Paul J. Sutton 224c, 224br; Phil Schermeister 227b, 248tr; R. W Jones 309; Richard Morrell 189bc; Rick Doyle 241ctr; Robert Holmes 97br, 277ctc; Roger Ressmeyer 169tr; Russ Schleipman 229; The Purcell Team 211ctr; Vince Streano 194t; Wally McNamee 220br, 220bcl, 224bl; Wavebreak Media LTD 191bc; Yann Arhus-Bertrand 249tl; **Demetrio Carrasco / Dorling Kindersley (c) Herge / Les Editions Casterman:** 112ccl; **Dorling Kindersley:** Banbury Museum 35c; Five Napkin Burger 152t; **Dixons:** 270cl, 270cr, 270bl, 270bcl, 270bcr, 270ccr; **Dreamstime.com:** Alexander Podshivalov 179tr, 191cr; Alexxl66 268tl; Andersastphoto 176tcl; Andrey Popov 191bl; Arne9001 190tl; Chaoss 26c; Designsstock 269cl; Monkey Business Images 26clb; Paul Michael Hughes 162tr; Serghei Starus 190bc; **Education Photos:** John Walmsley 26tl; **Empics Ltd:** Adam Day 236br; Andy Heading 243c; Steve White 249cbc; **Getty Images:** 48bcl, 100t, 114bcr, 154bl, 287tr; 94tr; Don Farrall / Digital Vision 176c; Ethan Miller 270bl; Inti St Clair 179bl; Liam Norris 188br; Sean Justice / Digital Vision 24br; **Dennis Gilbert:** 106tc; **Hulsta:** 70t; **Ideal Standard Ltd:** 72r; **The Image Bank/Getty Images:** 58; **Impact Photos:** Eliza Armstrong 115cr; Philip Achache 246t; **The Interior Archive:** Henry Wilson, Alfie's Market 114bl; Luke White, Architect: David Mikhail, 59tl; Simon Upton, Architect: Phillippe Starck, St Martins Lane Hotel 100bcr, 100br; **iStockphoto.com:** asterix0597 163tl; EdStock 190br; RichLegg 26bc; SorinVidis 27cr; **Jason Hawkes Aerial Photography:** 216t; **Dan Johnson:** 35r; **Kos Pictures Source:** 215cbl, 240tc, 240tr; David Williams 216b; **Lebrecht Collection:** Kate Mount 169bc; **MP Visual.com:** Mark Swallow 202t; **NASA:** 280cr, 280ccl, 281tl; **P&O Princess Cruises:** 214bl; **P A Photos:** 181br; **The Photographers' Library:** 186bl, 186bc, 186t; **Plain and Simple Kitchens:** 66t; **Powerstock Photolibrary:** 169tl, 256t, 287tc; **PunchStock:** Image Source 195tr; **Rail Images:** 208c, 208 cbl, 209br; **Red Consultancy:** Odeon cinemas 257br; **Redferns:** 259br; Nigel Crane 259c; **Rex

Features:** 106br, 259tc, 259tr, 259bl, 280b; Charles Ommaney 114tcr; J.F.F Whitehead 243cl; Patrick Barth 101tl; Patrick Frilet 189cbl; Scott Wiseman 287bl; **Royalty Free Images:** Getty Images/Eyewire 154bl; **Science & Society Picture Library:** Science Museum 202b; **Science Photo Library:** IBM Research 190cla; NASA 281cr; **SuperStock:** Ingram Publishing 62; Juanma Aparicio / age fotostock 172t; Nordic Photos 269tl; **Skyscan:** 168t, 182c, 298; Quick UK Ltd 212; **Sony:** 268bc; **Robert Streeter:** 154br; **Neil Sutherland:** 82tr, 83tl, 90t, 118, 188ctr, 196tl, 196tr, 299cl, 299bl; **The Travel Library:** Stuart Black 264t; **Travelex:** 97cl; **Vauxhall:** Technik 198t, 199tl, 199tr, 199cl, 199cr, 199ctcl, 199tcr, 199tcl, 199tcr, 200; **View Pictures:** Dennis Gilbert, Architects: ACDP Consulting, 106t; Dennis Gilbert, Chris Wilkinson Architects, 209tr; Peter Cook, Architects: Nicholas Crimshaw and partners, 208t; **Betty Walton:** 185br; **Colin Walton:** 2, 4, 7, 9, 10, 28, 42, 56, 92, 95c, 99tl, 99tcl, 102, 116, 120t, 138t, 146, 150t, 160, 170, 191ctcl, 192, 218, 252, 260br, 260l, 261tr, 261c, 261cr, 271cbl, 271cbr, 271ctcl, 278, 287br, 302, 401.

DK PICTURE LIBRARY:

Akhil Bahkshi; Patrick Baldwin; Geoff Brightling; British Museum; John Bulmer; Andrew Butler; Joe Cornish; Brian Cosgrove; Andy Crawford and Kit Hougton; Philip Dowell; Alistair Duncan; Gables; Bob Gathany; Norman Hollands; Kew Gardens; Peter James Kindersley; Vladimir Kozlik; Sam Lloyd; London Northern Bus Company Ltd; Tracy Morgan; David Murray and Jules Selmes; Musée Vivant du Cheval, France; Museum of Broadcast Communications; Museum of Natural History; NASA; National History Museum; Norfolk Rural Life Museum; Stephen Oliver; RNLI; Royal Ballet School; Guy Ryecart; Science Museum; Neil Setchfield; Ross Simms and the Winchcombe Folk Police Museum; Singaporte Symphony Orchestra; Smart Museum of Art; Tony Souter; Erik Svensson and Jeppe Wikstrom; Sam Tree of Keygrove Marketing Ltd; Barrie Watts; Alan Williams; Jerry Young.

Additional Photography by Colin Walton.

Colin Walton would like to thank:
A&A News, Uckfield; Abbey Music, Tunbridge Wells; Arena Mens Clothing, Tunbridge Wells; Burrells of Tunbridge Wells; Gary at Di Marco's; Jeremy's Home Store, Tunbridge Wells; Noakes of Tunbridge Wells; Ottakar's, Tunbridge Wells; Selby's of Uckfield; Sevenoaks Sound and Vision; Westfield, Royal Victoria Place, Tunbridge Wells.

All other images © Dorling Kindersley
For further information see: www.dkimages.com

español • english